BECOMING YOUR DREAMS

BECOMING YOUR DREAMS

Scott V. Black
and Chris Carey

published by

CREATIVE
communication
PUBLICATIONS
Atlanta, Georgia USA

Written by Scott V. Black and Chris Carey

Edited by M. Kay duPont

Cover concept and design by Troy Arnold and Scott V. Black
Interior illustrations and typography by Chris Carey

DISCLAIMER: The purpose of this book is to provide insights regarding motivation, personal improvement, and leadership skills in the workplace. It is not meant to replace professional counsel for legal or financial matters, or for emotional or psychological issues. Referral to a competent business consultant, or to a qualified counselor or therapist, is recommended for use outside the scope of this publication, which is intended for general use and not as a specific course of treatment.

Published by CreativeCommunication Publications
Post Office Box 725245 Atlanta, Georgia 31139

Printed in the United States of America

First Edition – May, 2003

ISBN: 0-9709307-3-9

TABLE OF CONTENTS

Jeff Justice explains why reading this book will be a life-challenging experience—and possibly a life-changing one if you let it!

What do you really want out of life and why do you want it? It's not as obvious as you might think!

Everything is created first in the mind and then in the physical world. Powerless thoughts and words create a powerless world!

To live the life of your dreams, you have to lead it. Learn to take possession of your dreams every day!

Unleash the power of emotional intelligence to power your dreams and plans. Learn to pursue life and leadership with Passion!

You can lose money and regain it, but you can never make up lost time. Make the most of your moments with Focus!

Uncover what's been holding you back from succeeding as you want to. Learn the secret of no-holds-barred Commitment!

Understand the strengths and weaknesses of your team if you want to win. Success is a team sport!

FOREWORD

The first time I saw Scott Black, he was onstage at the Mandalay Bay Hotel & Casino in Las Vegas, delivering a keynote presentation to the top salespeople in Cingular Wireless, where I also was speaking. Many in the audience had already attended his "Empower U" leadership programs and were singing his praises.

Three months later, I was invited to participate in Empower U's *Leadership Awakening* program and started a journey that will influence the rest of my life.

Scott Black is a master of the mind–body connection, aligning what you truly want with what you really do. His methods will help you gain a solid understanding of that connection, showing you how to *create* and *live* your life the way you were meant to—instead of just reacting as things happen to you.

When you adopt the three principles that Scott reveals in this book, the world will become a better place *because of you.* How powerful is that? You'll discover what you really want in life, and you'll make your dreams a reality. You'll watch them come true in your career and in your personal life.

It's important to caution you about the exercises Scott has placed in this book. It would be easy to skip over them in order to "get through" the book quickly. Don't cheat yourself! They are part of Scott's dynamic process, and they'll take you to places in the heart you may not have visited for a long time. Take the time, do it right, and you'll *become your dreams!*

You just have to *Want It! Create It! Live It!*

Be Happy!

Jeff Justice, CSP, CLL
"Humor" Resources Director

Jeff Justice is a Certified Speaking Professional, the highest earned designation of the National Speakers Association. He is the author of *How To Ad Lib Like A Professional (Or Just Look Like One).* Jeff's workshops and seminars on using appropriate humor to positively impact workplace interaction have been featured on CNN and CNBC. He says, "If you're attempting to manage others without using humor, you're like the guy who cuts the grass at the cemetery: you have a lot of people underneath you but no one's paying attention!"

INTRODUCTION

Hello. I'm Scott Black.

I'm guessing that you're reading this book because you're interested in improving your life. Maybe you're even a motivation-junkie, and you collect books on self-improvement.

If you and I really *could* improve all by ourselves, there would be no need for *"self*-improvement" books and programs. The truth is, we all need "outside" sources of feedback and encouragement to help us improve.

For this reason, there are hundreds of "guru" books written and published every year by authors who hold themselves up as prime examples to follow. To tell you the truth, I don't fit the guru pattern. I'm not six-and-a-half-feet tall with perfect, snow-white teeth. I don't hold advanced degrees in business management, industrial psychology, and international relations. I don't even have my own infomercial…yet!

Instead, I'm an "average guy" who learned lots of life's most valuable lessons the hard way. I struggle to be a little less of a hypocrite every day—to really "walk the talk." That's how I became "above average" and am today a sought-after corporate consultant and trainer, and founder of Empower U, Incorporated. I lead a team of skilled trainers and facilitators who teach "leadership in motion" to companies and individuals all over North America.

I've recorded many life lessons in this book. You'll identify with them because they are time-tested and reliable. I'll tell you the truth in these pages and promise the lessons will work for you...if you will work at them.

Maybe you're just the opposite of a self-improvement fan. You think "motivation" is a waste of time because you gave it a shot once or twice and didn't like it. Or because some "experts" *say* one thing in a seminar and then *do* things very differently in real life. Or they push complicated formulas for success that just might work for you—if only you could find your seminar notes when you need to remember them!

Relax. You'll feel at home with this book. It focuses on only *three* requirements for succeeding in your *personal* life, and they are also necessary for true *professional* success. Yes, it *is* worth your time to read John Maxwell's *The 21 Irrefutable Laws of Leadership,* Stephen Covey's *The 7 Habits of Highly Successful People,* even Dr. Laura's *Ten Stupid Things Women Do to Mess Up Their Lives,* but this book concentrates on just *three* things to do in order to *be* your dreams.

First, you have to *want* it. Do you know what you really want out of your life? You'll see it more clearly when you've finished this book. But *wanting* it isn't enough—you also have to *create* it. That's the second thing. Our world is full of wannabes and dreamers who never make it real. So, the third and final step is to *Live It*. We're talking about more than achieving and accomplishing for personal power and recognition here. You really can live your dreams in such a way that the world will be better tomorrow because you were here today. When I think about that, every day becomes for me "a great day to be alive!"

Perhaps making such claims for this book sounds egotistical to you. Let me explain why I can confidently promise results. We have built our training and consulting business on word-of-mouth recommendations from people like you who have attended our seminars and experienced such profound improvements in their lives that friends and coworkers ask what has happened! Our seminar attendance grows and grows, because people want to experience what they have seen happen in their friends.

Honestly, it's impossible to bring the seminar experience to life in a book. However, much of the material in *Becoming Your Dreams: Want It! Create It! Live It!* is drawn from our three-day *Leadership Awakening* program. This information will start you on a parallel path as you experience many dimensions of those training sessions.

Some people feel a course like *Leadership Awakening* would not apply to them since they are not recognized as leaders. In our three-day course, these individuals recognize their own great capacity to lead, encourage, and develop others through an example of empowered living.

This book will also help those who have experienced *Leadership Awakening* to explain some of it to their friends. It's not that we tell anyone to keep the processes a secret, but our graduates have difficulty explaining what happens because much of it is personal and unique to them. It's not *what* we do that's so powerful—it's the *way* we do it. Also, most people who experience *Leadership Awakening* really hope their family, friends, and coworkers will attend, and they want to preserve the discoveries for them.

At the very least, *Becoming Your Dreams* will provide common ground for those who have and have not experienced *Leadership Awakening*.

In transferring our concepts to print, I have enlisted the help of my friend, Chris Carey, who is a successful author and speaker in his own right. Last year, Chris experienced *Leadership Awakening* and the follow-up *Leadership Adventure*—not just as an assignment connected to coauthoring this book, but to experience the *personal benefits* of the courses. I appreciate his communication skills, but even more, I value his commitment to living an empowered life.

My coworkers and staff at Empower U, and even our graduates, have freely shared experiences and insights as we've worked to make this book a solid resource and reference tool for you. Thank you, Team, for your commitment to excellence as you model an empowered life in the seminars and in your daily lives.

I would be remiss if I failed to thank Butch and Susan Anderson, and Brett and Karen Wassell, who believed in me and supported me in gaining financial assistance when no one else was willing to step over the line. Also, to my "pseudo" big brother, Jim Ashworth, and his wife Nancy, thank you for helping me in ways I couldn't even begin to acknowledge with mere words.

I also thank our corporate clients, including those who "took a risk" when our name and concepts were untested: Coca-Cola, Nabisco, Kraft, Cintas, CompuCom, Tony's Fine Foods, Lahonton Golf Club, Nugget Markets, Delta Dental, Cingular Wireless, Michelin, The Dwyer Group, American Athletic, Baylor Health Care System Foundation, the Army National Guard, and many others.

We have designed our seminars and this book to provide *life-challenging* experiences. They can become *life-changing* experiences if you allow yourself to join in... With Passion...Heart...Body...and Soul!

Scott V Black

Reno, Nevada

Thanks, Scott, for the opportunity to share a few words in my own voice as we tell the Empower U story in print. I appreciate your invitation to assist in transforming the lives of readers as they awaken and learn the secrets of impactful leadership.

The real reason I'm glad for this introductory opportunity is to encourage you, our reader, that very positive progress is possible in your life if you'll "trust the process" as you read this book.

When my friend Rick Herceg nominated me to attend the *Leadership Awakening* seminar, I went because of his strong endorsement. He told me two things before I left: "Trust the process" and "You'll understand it all in due time." Rick meant that I should keep an open, active mind while I was in the sessions, but that I shouldn't try to "figure it out" before permitting myself to participate in it. That was great advice, and I pass it on to you.

This page also provides an opportunity for me to brag on Scott Black. He's a strong personality and a demanding leader who doesn't lower the bar on anything in life. He lives, eats, sleeps, and breathes accomplishment and achievement. Yet, he is humble and eager to continue learning and growing in life. Scott's passion is helping others discover life's success secrets. He's for *real,* and so are the truths you will read in this book.

Atlanta, Georgia

SECTION I:
3 STEPS TO
BECOMING
YOUR DREAMS

"It must be borne in mind that the tragedy of life doesn't lie in not reaching your goal. The tragedy lies in having no goal to reach. It isn't a calamity to die with dreams unfulfilled, but it is a calamity not to dream. It is not a disaster to be unable to capture your ideal, but it is a disaster to have no ideal to capture. It is not a disgrace not to reach the stars, but it is a disgrace to have no stars to reach for. Not failure, but low aim, is a sin."

— Dr. Benjamin Mayes

CHAPTER 1:
WANT IT!

"What do you want?" You've been hearing that question since you were a little kid, wandering through the house calling for Mom.

Up until now, when someone asked you what you want, their question may really have meant, "Why are you bothering me?" Or "Get to the bottom line! Can't you see I'm busy?"

You've heard it when ordering food or drinks at a restaurant. You may have said it impatiently when asking a child to quickly decide what flavor ice cream cone to get while standing in line. Often, "What do you want?" can mean "Just choose *something.*" Not this time.

What do you really want?

Right now, the *real* question I'm asking you has a lot more importance, and your choices aren't based on a limited selection. You need not choose from only "A," "B," or "C."

I'm not asking you about your *immediate* needs or desires—what will satisfy you for the moment. I'm asking, "Tell me what you want, what you *really, really* want!" Judging from the

17

title of this book, you can guess it's not a trivial question. *What you want* is going to be the core of this book. And you'll see how you can get it.

Not how, but why

In one of his seminars, my coauthor, Chris Carey, tells how Sears sold over a million quarter-inch drill bits last year to customers who didn't even *want* to purchase a drill bit. What they really wanted was a quarter-inch hole—the drill bit was just a way to get it.

Drill bits really ask a *how* question. They tell *how* you intend to get a hole, but they offer no answer about *why* you want a hole in the first place. Even why you want the hole isn't the real issue. The real question is: What are you planning to do with the hole once you have it?

Is the hole going to allow you to hang a picture frame? Will it make a pilot hole so you can screw two objects together? Are you looking for termites in your foundation? Do you want to drain water in a leaky ceiling? Are you replacing a wood-joining plug while repairing a chair? Getting rid of a rivet? Creating a design in the metal sides of a pie safe? Making space for a peep-hole in your front door?

So, when I ask you what you want, think

in terms of *why,* not *how* or *if it is possible* to accomplish it.

Internal motivators

Let's not think about what you're willing to *settle* for, or what you think you *need* in order to obtain a temporary, short-term desire. What we're after is identifying your internal *why.*

For example, many people say they want more money, while what they *really* want is what they think the money will get for them. Their real *why* could be personal freedom, time with family, love, happiness, security, power, acknowledgment. One thing is sure: they're not after stacks of green paper.

Sometimes it's easier to identify what you *don't* want. "I *don't* want to be trapped in a dead-end job!" Or, "I *don't* want to live in fear of the future!" Or, "I *don't* want to eat brussels sprouts ever again in my life!" (Sorry, just a personal note.) It's often true that we have to deal with the things we *don't* want because we have not been clear enough about the things we *do* want. You may know more about what you wish to avoid than what you want to pursue.

What are you after? What do you *want?* Do you have an idea *why* you want it? What is your internal *why?* When you understand *what* you

19

want and *why* getting it is so important to you, you'll find yourself closer to getting it—and better prepared to handle it once it's yours.

You're about to participate in a *Leadership Awakening* exercise that helps our students identify what they really want. First, let's take a look at *why* we're doing it, so you'll understand where we're headed. Then you'll be less likely to skip past it and miss its benefits to your life. (This is a distinct advantage for you, because we don't provide reasons prior to doing things at *Leadership Awakening*. Instead, we tell participants "all will be known in due time," and their sponsor asks them simply to "trust the process.")

The reason behind this exercise is that each of us has a "polite" list of *What I Want*. You began tentatively voicing yours as you discovered needs and goals. If no one threw their hands up in alarm and shrieked, "Oh, no! Not that!," you decided it was a good, safe thing to want. Over time it has become what you tell yourself and others, because it sounds good, but it may no longer fit with the real who, what, when, where, why, and how of your life.

When you reexamine your wants, you may find that what you used to want is no longer big enough for the person you have become. In doing this inventory, you may discover a real want that is bigger than the person you are right now. Our students often realize that what they truly want has little in common with the way they are living their lives.

Get out of your head

So *what do you want?* In our seminar setting, student *A* asks student *B,* rapidly and repeatedly, "What do you want?" Student *B* rapidly responds, "I want..." and fills in the blank. Before the words are complete, student *A* is demanding again, "What do you want?", and student *B* must respond with a totally different answer.

But before those words are finished, student *A* is again asking, "What do you want? What do you want?" And student *B* must give a totally different reply. Is *A* not listening to what *B* has been saying? No, not really. What *B* wants doesn't depend on *A's* approval. It's none of *A's* business what *B* wants! It shouldn't matter to *A* at all right now. The real motivation in asking is that it *should* matter to *B.*

At first, *What I Want* comes from your polite list. It's the safe, edited stuff. It's like asking a beauty contestant about her dreams and hearing her respond, "Peace in our world." No one is surprised, and the audience applauds lightly, but you know it isn't so. She's not a *contestant* for world peace. More honestly, peace would be nice, but she's dreaming of fame, a publicity tour, and a Corvette!

Likewise, your *real* wants might not come out on the first go-around, or on the second or third. Typically, we ask, "What do you want?" in 30-second bursts. And then we switch, so *B* asks and *A* answers. And we do it again and again. It's mentally and physically exhausting as more and more of the "fluff" falls away.

We tend to be analytical creatures, living on the left side of our brains—the more verbal, logical side. I want you to jump the track and work with your right side—the more intuitive, creative, emotional side.

Finally, everything boils down to what you *really* want, and for some, it's a revelation. "Why did I say that?" Because it was in your *heart*, not in your head! Jesus said, "It is out of the *abundance of the heart* that the mouth speaks" *(Luke 6:45)*. Yet most of us are not listening to our hearts. We're listening to our heads.

Most of our students are far too cerebral when they go through this exercise, and you'll probably start that way, too. You'll need to get out of your head and into your heart. If you don't struggle in this effort to discover your real motivations, you haven't dug deep enough. If you're not surprised as you respond, you're still playing it safe in your head and not playing loose with your heart. (As you'll see later, a great life is "born" in hot passion, not in cold reason. Trust this process!) Challenge yourself as *Leadership Awakening* would challenge you. Don't settle for your polite list anymore. Discover what you *really* want.

EXERCISE #1

Here is a description of your first task. Read it now, until you get to the words, *STOP HERE*. Then go no further until you have actually completed this exercise.

In any self-directed book, there is a tendency to read through quickly, just to see where it is heading. But this book is a *process,* and if you pick and choose what you will do and when you will do it, you'll short-change the worthwhile results that are on their way to you.

Respect what we have designed this exercise to create in your life—and respect your capacity to complete it.

The first thing you'll need is a notebook and a pen or pencil. There is room in the margins of this book for notes you want to remember, but you will need an uncensored place where you can write your thoughts during this (and other) exercises, from which you can later tear out pages if you wish. Your notes will provide a way to write without "editing" your ideas as they come to you.

Second, you'll need to find a spot where you can be alone. You won't get the results you're after if you can't get off by yourself, away from people you are accustomed to "performing" for. You don't need anyone's permission or approval in this exercise. You need to find out what you really want. So go where no one will be listening to you or evaluating what comes from your time alone.

Once you are in your private spot, note the time. Open your notebook to a blank sheet of paper, and at the top, write: "I want...."

Then, for three full minutes, "rush-write" what you want. "Rush-writing" means that you just write and write and write and write. You don't stop, you don't edit—you don't even think about whether you're writing things that make sense. You just write, letting it flow. Don't write "because" sentences that will send you back into your head. There's no need to justify your thoughts. Just put your pen on the paper and don't take it off unless you have to. *Do this now!*

— STOP HERE —
*Go no further until you complete
Exercise #1. Then continue reading.*

No fooling—did you do it? You're establishing a pattern for the rest of this book by how you respond to the first exercise! If you were tempted to keep *reading* without *doing,* think again. How you handle this book is a metaphor for how you handle life. If you short-change this process, what other opportunities in your life are you short-changing?

Leadership Awakening participants hear over and over, "The way you respond to this training is exactly the way you respond in your personal and business lives. The faces and situations change, but we are creatures of habit." Like my coach used to say, the way you practice is the way you play. Where else in life are you letting down, giving up, falling short, failing to raise the bar?

Give yourself a chance to make a change, to make a difference. If you skipped the exercise, go back and do it now. You won't have a second opportunity to get this right.

Once more with feeling

When your three minutes of rush-writing is up, stop. Take a few deep breaths and let go of the tension you may be feeling. Don't reread your notes yet. Just take a breather, shake out your writer's cramp, and get ready to do it once more. Chances are, you've just begun to get out of your head and into your heart. This was the warm-up. You won't improve what you've written by running it through your brain again. Trust this process! Check your time again. Fill up at least one full page as you spend another three minutes rush-writing "I want..." once more. *Do it now!*

— STOP HERE —
*Go no further until you complete
the exercise. Then continue reading.*

Again, did you finish your assignment, or did you skip over it? Remember, how you handle this book is a metaphor for how you handle your life. Where else do you have a "do-it-later" mentality? Where else are you just scanning the pages, grabbing a piece but missing the big picture? When you have completed both steps in **Exercise #1**, we can look together at what you've learned.

What did you learn?

At least two factors should have become apparent in your writing. One is the number of things you wrote down—how long your list became as you "uncorked" your stuffed-up wants.

The other factor is the actual contents of your list. Were you surprised at some of the things you wrote down? They may not have occurred to you consciously before, and when they popped out on paper, you may have wondered, "Where did *that* come from?"

You're "becoming aware of being unaware." Perhaps you've been looking without seeing, hearing without listening, touching without feeling. Your rush-writing allowed your true desires to bubble to the surface. You made the longest journey of your life: the 12 inches between your head and your heart.

Right now, I'm recalling some of the *wants* participants have shared with me over the years of conducting *Leadership Awakening* classes. Once, "Phil," a reserved CPA, burst out with, "I want my father to be proud of me!" He was startled because his father had died long before, and his "practical" side never would have thought of it.

"Why did I say that?," Phil asked. There could be several reasons:

1. They say you're never a man until your father says you are. Maybe Phil really wanted his dad's validation, even though it would

27

not be heard from beyond the grave.

2. Phil was to become a father for the first time in a few months, and he really wanted to be the same kind of father for his child as the man he had looked up to in his youth.

3. Perhaps Phil had a desire to make amends for youthful mistakes. There are always things we would like an opportunity to do over again, but life can be lived only in forward motion, never in reverse.

Actually, the reason Phil said it isn't as important as the fact that he did say it. The same is true for you at this stage of your "I want…" discovery. Be careful of asking yourself *why* in relation to these *wants*. You can get yourself stuck in value judgments, which is not where you *want* to be at this point.

Simply put, what's on your list offers some insights into what you *really* want, but your greatest benefit is that you learned you do have wants—even *needs*—you might not have considered…up until now.

Creative discontent

A benefit of developing a *want* list is "creative discontent." "Destructive discontent" creates greed and envy, selfishness and turmoil. Its aim is to get a "bigger piece of the pie" by cutting out smaller pieces for everyone else. "Creative discontent" is healthy and may show that you don't want a piece of the pie at all—maybe what you really want is strawberry shortcake!

You must have a sense of discontent with where you are at this point in your life. It's sometimes called creative *tension*. It gives you a reason to get up in the morning, do what you do, go home at night, and get up the next morning to do it again and again and again. No, not living in a rut, but working toward something that makes a difference—being a better spouse or salesperson, achieving recognition, getting a reward. Without creative discontent, humans never take action to get out of their ruts or move away from their comfort zones.

In an old Southern story, a hound dog is stretched out on the porch of a country cabin. Once in a while, he lifts his head and lets out a pitiful howl. Then he lays his head down and looks forlorn until the next time he lifts it to moan. A visiting neighbor asks the dog's owner why the dog does this all day long. The owner says, "He's sittin' on a nail stickin' up from the porch...."

"Well, why don't he move?" the neighbor asks. "That's there's his favorite spot," the owner replies, "and it don't hurt enough to move, just enough to complain about it!"

Until your discontent leads you to *action,* you may experience a sense of being on auto-pilot or just going through the motions. This is often accompanied by complacency or inatten-tion, and no lasting change can occur. Discontent can wake you up and make you move off *your* nail! So what do you want?

What do you value?

Research into why people do what they do often centers on *values.* I'm not thinking about religion or morality. I'm asking about what you value and believe is important in your life.

This value question is loaded with traps. Your answer is not going to be as easy as, "Well, I value my relationship with my spouse...." That's nice—along with world peace and a Corvette!

Research on people's behavior shows that what they *value* heavily influences what they *want.* German philosopher Dr. Eduard Spranger observed six attitudes through which individu-als value the world, and in his ground-breaking book, *Types of Men,* published in 1928, he pro-claimed that these attitudes define the *why* of our behavior. Spranger showed us how we move into action based on what we value. We pursue what we value and discount what we don't.

Our values (meaning *what* we value) also influence us to be negative or indifferent toward people and experiences when their values are different from our own. Behavioral researchers Judy Suiter and Bill Bonstetter have made a career of studying and interpreting the *value* of values, including how they affect our personal interests and attitudes. We don't want to get off-course, but let's identify what these value bases are so you can see where your discontent and wants come from. The six value descriptions are:

- Theoretical
- Aesthetic
- Individualistic
- Utilitarian
- Social
- Traditional

Psychologists have developed numerous "values and attitudes" lists, but these six are used most widely to provide insights into our individual motivations, especially in business, whether we are male or female. An individual's top two values significantly influence how they decide what's important and worthy of pursuit.

Valuing the Theoretical view

People with high theoretical attitude want to discover *truth* and *knowledge.* They employ objective reasoning and reject emotional, subjective arguments (and people). They have a high interest in solving problems, conducting research, and asking questions. They enjoy "learning for the sake of learning" and get so bogged down in details that they may neglect practical action.

Valuing the Utilitarian view

People with a high utilitarian attitude are driven by *usefulness* and *return on investment*. How time and money are allocated is a primary focus with a very practical view. They maximize their time, talent, and resources (both personal and professional) to reach their potential. This bottom-line profit perspective often causes them to be viewed as self-centered.

Valuing the Aesthetic view

People with a high aesthetic attitude seek *beauty* and *balance, form* and *harmony*. Self-realization, or actualization, and attainment of the higher self are their strong motivators. They tend to see events subjectively, and use their own experience as a test of validity, as opposed to a more practical, objective approach. They are their own "frame of reference."

Valuing the Social view

People with a high social attitude are often described as *unselfish, sympathetic,* and *kind.* Their time, talent, and resources are often dedicated to eliminating conflict and hate, even on a global scale. They tend to view theoretical, utilitarian, and aesthetic styles as indifferent and cold. Even to their own detriment, they adopt others' problems as their responsibility to resolve.

Valuing the Individualistic view

People with a high *individualist* attitude are motivated by personal advancement and positions of power. Their goals are victory and self-assertion, as they seek to control the destiny of themselves and others. Their decisions and actions are strategic, and they form key alliances to accomplish their agenda. They do not think in terms of "team" decisions, but of "soldiers" carrying out orders.

Valuing the Traditional view

People with a high *traditional* attitude are motivated by their guiding principles. Their "faith" can often be more in their belief itself, rather than in facts. Consistency in action and application is key, often accompanied with great passion. They may see situations as "black and white," and may be seen as rigid and dogmatic. True to their beliefs, they "walk their talk."

We'll come back to the *value* question later,

33

as we consider the effectiveness of your leadership skills. For now, just consider how your own list of "I want...." has been influenced by what you value. Just because something showed up on your list does not indicate that you need to pursue that particular *want* as an all-encompassing life goal. As you mature in the process of *being your dreams,* you'll see how to appreciate what others *value* and include them in your approach.

What others want

In a speech I gave recently at a Cingular Wireless sales leadership convention, I asked, "How do you know what your clients want? What makes them happy? And how do you know when you haven't connected with a client?"

I told this audience that one of our biggest challenges in working with other people is that they don't respond to *reality*. What they see and respond to is their own version, or "map," of reality—what's real to them. Our reality is based on our perceptions, our filters. Simply giving people what would please and motivate you is not the same as finding out what they want.

Let me give you a real-life example. This story came from "Fred" at the Dwyer Group in

Texas. (Whenever I identify a client company by name, it's accurate, but I've disguised people because we are all "Leaders Under Construction.")

When Fred and his wife were first married, he often gave her roses to show his love. He told me that, as a kid, he watched his dad bring roses to his mom, who always responded with warmth and love. But when Fred brought home roses, he received a very different response. His wife became distant and cold.

As he discussed this with their marriage counselor, the reason for her reaction became clear. His wife explained that, as she was growing up, her father cheated many times on her mother and, after each affair, he would bring his wife flowers. So did a bouquet from her own husband mean love to her? Not at all. It signaled betrayal. Her experience provided a very different map of reality and she followed it to a different destination.

Just as sensitively as you are learning to ask yourself and listen to what you want, you will learn how to ask questions and listen to responses to know what others want. As Zig Ziglar teaches, "You can have anything you want in life if you'll just help enough other people get what they want."

BECOMING YOUR DREAMS

NOTES TO
MYSELF

Go for what you value

So, what do you want? My associates and I ask each other this question all the time. And since we understand the concept of *values,* we know we don't feel much fulfillment by achieving something we don't value.

You could be correct in telling your spouse or coworkers all of their character flaws. You could also destroy those relationships. What do you want, to be right or to have right relationships?

Jesus asked, "What shall it profit a man if he gains the whole world and loses his own soul?" *(Mark 8:36).* In applying His wisdom to this topic, I ask you, "What if you got what you wanted but it wasn't what you wanted after all?"

Is what you're doing actually bringing you what you want? Is the outcome truly going to be worthwhile? If not, it's time to align what you *say* is important to you with what you're *doing* to create it. It's time to pick yourself up, dust yourself off, and hit it again!

You've probably heard that the definition of insanity is doing the same thing over and over but expecting a different result.

Have you been lying on a nail in enough pain to complain, but, up until now, not in enough pain to move? You will make one of two

36

decisions by the end of this book: to either get
moving or stop howling.

No one can force you to do anything sug-
gested in these pages. Some readers have already
proven that by skipping **Exercise #1**, and still
attempting to make sense of what follows. (No
one's looking over your shoulder, so if that's you,
take a few minutes to catch up on **Exercise #1**.
By now, I hope you understand that this is not a
process you've *got* to do, but one you *get* to do.)

Unlike our *Leadership Awakening* classes,
there is no peer pressure or instructor team looking over your shoulder and challenging you to
finish the course. You are a volunteer. If you've
read this far already, it's because you really *want*
to improve some part of your life. I applaud you.

Samurai warriors went into battle wearing
armor over the fronts of their bodies, but wore
no protection on their backs. Why? Because they
gave their word—their *Bushido*—that they would
never turn and run. "No armor on the back" meant
every action moved them forward to victory.

Are you living your life in a forward direction? As we take this journey together, can you
live like a Samurai, with no armor on the back?
Is your life worthy of this commitment?

When you live your life like it matters, it
does! Now...*what do you want?*

"The future is not a result of choices among alternative paths offered by the present, but a place that is created—created *first* in mind and will, created *next* in activity. The future is not some place we are going to, but one we are creating. The paths are not to be found, but made, and the activity of making them changes both the maker and the destination."

— John Schaar

CHAPTER 2:
CREATE IT!

NOTES TO
MYSELF

If you were building your "dream home," one of the first things you'd want is the architect's blueprint, right? It's the same with your other dreams too. You get to be the architect! What type of future are you building through the blueprint of your wants? Remember, when you live your life like it matters, it does!

Life is really about asking the right questions. If you ask the right questions, you can get the right answers. We began by asking, "What do you want?" I must warn you that it's a lifetime question. You'll revisit it often to make sure you are on track to becoming your dreams. In this chapter, we'll consider the second step: *Create It.*

When you have a handle on what you want, you need to make it real. What will your dream *look* like, *sound* like, *feel* like, *smell* and *taste* like? (Did the last two surprise you? What about the *"sweet taste* of victory"? Have you ever hesitated to act because "something *smells fishy"?)*

How will you know when you reach your dream if you can't supply these sensory answers?

BECOMING YOUR DREAMS

Have you ever been to Hershey, Pennsylvania? Can you guess how you would know if you were getting close? Even the outskirts of town smell like chocolate! So what will *your* success look, sound, feel, smell, and taste like as you near it?

Recognize it when you see it

Would you know you were at your own house if you had amnesia? You wouldn't, because you'd have no idea what "home" should look like, sound like, etc.

I was doing a follow-up session with one of our Coca-Cola executive clients, and "Tom" shared with me that his wife was upset about his "transformation" after attending our classes. He'd begun attending to her needs, writing poetry for her, bathing the kids, becoming more expressive in his spiritual life. I asked, "What's wrong with that?" He said, "She's been telling me to do these things for 10 years!"

When I spoke with Tom's wife, I discovered what was wrong. She had wanted them to go to a "couples class" at church to change him. She actually got the result she had wanted for so long—a changed husband—but she didn't know she was "home" because she hadn't "been there" ahead of time. She didn't know what it would take to "Create It!" Here's the key: we always do everything twice, first in our mind's eye and then in reality. Again, would you know you were at your own house if you had amnesia? What does "home" look like?

The process of *creating* can be lengthy, because it involves stages. Let's say a little girl wants to grow some sunflowers in a garden. With an adult's guidance and knowledge, she plants her seeds in soil. She adds just the right amount of fertilizer and water, then she sits down to watch and wait. Her sunflowers aren't going to bloom in five minutes, are they? Not in five hours and not in five days! What will happen if she digs them up every hour to see why they haven't sprouted yet? They never will! It takes time to grow, and when the sunflowers first sprout, they won't even look like flowers to her untrained eyes. That's often what it's like when you go about *creating what you want*.

Cultivate your dreams

There are steps you take in *Becoming Your Dreams* while you wait for them to sprout and then to bloom. You plant your dream in fertile soil, give it "food" to grow, provide the "light" and "water" that it needs. You pull up the "weeds" that threaten its support system, and you protect it from "parasites." You understand that, beneath the surface, out of your sight, germination is taking place. And you remind yourself how it will *look, sound, feel, smell,* and *taste* when your dream blooms.

Have you ever pictured your *goals* as tender shoots waiting to blossom? What about your plans to work out and get into the shape of those models who sell exercise equipment on TV? What about your plans to lose weight, learn Spanish, buy a specific car, or visit a certain place on vacation? In the past, when your "picture" of *exactly* what it would be like became dim and gray, that's when you dropped your dreams.

At Empower U, we teach goal-*getting,* not just goal-*setting.* Many people set goals rather than get goals because they begin at the wrong place. They start where they are instead of where they're going. Even if it defies your previous experience, you must start from where you want to end up, not where you are. Where you are now is littered with discouraging obstacles and excuses. Where you're going is filled with hopes and dreams. Someone said, "Obstacles are what you see when you take your eyes off your goals."

In the *Create It* stages of becoming your dreams, take really good care of your garden! "See" it regularly. What does it look like in full bloom? How bright are the colors? How sweet is the scent? It feels good to succeed and accomplish your goals. It makes all the difference between being a goal-*setter* and a goal-*getter!*

A map to get you there

Some people set goals and start their journey before they know where they are. How can they plan the path to their goal? If you were lost in a deep, thick forest of trees and had been walking for days, you wouldn't have a frame of reference for where you were. You might be only a hundred yards from emerging into a clearing or a highway without knowing it. And you would never get out if you thought, "Wait! I must be headed in the wrong direction. I'd better go back the other way."

Without knowing what the end result looks like, you would stumble and struggle on until luck provided a way out. However, people hovering high above you in a helicopter would have a clear perspective of the whole scene. They would see when you should turn and where you should go, because they could see the end.

Look at the maze puzzle on the following page. The challenge is to draw an uninterrupted line from the starting arrow to the keyhole shape in the center without crossing over any of the solid lines. In really complicated maze puzzles,

Start here, and help the key find the keyhole...

it's usually easier to begin at the end point and work your way back to the starting point. This is because, when you are starting out, you have several options to choose from. One will lead you to an opening and your next choice, while all others will eventually lead to a dead end. But when you work the puzzle backward, you avoid most dead ends, because every opening presents a good choice. Your end result is clear and your choices far less confusing when you work backward from your desired result.

Dr. Stephen Covey presents a similar success path in his book, *The 7 Habits of Highly Effective People.* He calls it "beginning with the end in mind." I call it "making a map." In our seminars, we talk about "the journey of a thousand miles." You know, the one that begins with a single step? We say that it begins with a single step and a map! You have to know where you want to end up in order to begin where you are.

Go to the very end of your dream, the goal, and create what it's going to *look, feel,* and *sound* like when you accomplish that goal. Then do an about-face: Work yourself back to where you are now, filling in all the gaps. You've marked out your path, set up trail markers, and created the map you can follow to your dream. You've identified the pattern that will get you *what you want!*

Everything is created twice

As I mentioned earlier, all things are created twice: first mentally, through vision, and then physically, in reality. This is one of those pesky, immutable, inviolable, eternal, universal laws. (You can't get around it!) So first envision the end result clearly.

Remember what happens when somebody wants to build a dream home? It all begins with identified *wants*. The individual begins with an idea, or a vision, of what this home should look like. From a description, the architect designs this ideal house on a blueprint, which is combined with the builder's plans before a single shovel of dirt is turned.

The house is already "constructed" in the homeowner's mind, and the architect's plans are laid out so this vision can be communicated to all of the builders who will work to create a house that matches the original dream. Blueprints allow the architect to transfer the vision and show others how it will be realized.

NOTES TO
MYSELF

The architect of your future

We must be the architects of our lives! You and I have to design our lives the way we want them to be, *creating* the life we *want*. If we fail to plan (from the end to the beginning), we will find ourselves living out someone else's plan. If we don't know where we're going, how will we know when we get there?

When my two children, Faith and Christian, were watching Disney's animated *Alice in Wonderland,* I saw a great illustration. Alice came to a fork in the road and stopped to consider which path to take. The Cheshire Cat appeared out of nowhere, and Alice asked, "Which road should I take?" The Cat asked the right question: "Where are you going?" Alice replied, "I don't know," and the Cat said, "Then any road will get you there!"

Who knows better than you what you want? Who, other than you, bears responsibility for what you do with what you have? Who, other than those you love, deserves to benefit most from what you accomplish in your life?

When you create a future that honors who you are and what you were created to do, you become an "on purpose" and unstoppable person. We'll think about this more when we get to the chapter on vision and purpose, but for now, understand that a person without purpose drifts. If you've been in the Pacific Northwest and seen salmon struggling their way through rapids and up cascading waterfalls, you sense that they *know* they have a purpose, a destiny in life. Dead fish float downstream; live salmon oppose all obstacles because they have places to go and things to do!

The late Lewis Grizzard, a Southern humorist and writer, said he learned from a dog sled team that, unless you're the lead dog, the view never changes! That's why our program is called *Leadership Awakening.* Unless you *wake up* and become the *leader* of your life, someone else will be the lead dog. And your view will always be the same: You'll be staring at the boss-dog's butt! (Okay, it's not *genteel,* but I think you'll remember it!) Remember, when you live your life like it matters, it does!

To create our future and take charge of our lives, we must not only create and articulate our *vision;* we also must create the *steps* necessary to accomplish it. As you and I plan our lives, we *create* our dreams!

What do you believe?

Your belief system is an important part of creating your dream. Like *values* in the last chapter, "beliefs" may not have the meaning you expect. We're not considering your religious or philosophical views. Rather, what do you believe about yourself? What are your current capabilities? What is your potential?

Do you believe you can change the ways you have thought and acted in the past? Are you willing to "reframe" your past successes and failures by saying, "That was then, this is now"?

Are you willing to accept responsibility for the past without locking yourself into insanity? Once again, insanity is doing the same thing over and over, but somehow expecting the results to be different. What have you believed in the past that has failed over and over again to provide expected results, yet you continue to believe it because it doesn't hurt enough yet to move?

Yesterday is history, tomorrow's a mystery, today is the present. Treat it like the gift it is! The time is *now*…to pick yourself up, dust yourself off, and hit it again.

Do you believe in your future, or do you believe in your excuses? Zig Ziglar says, "It's not your aptitude but your *attitude* that determines your *altitude.*" In other words, how far you go in life is greatly determined by how you see life—the "frame" you put around your experiences. Your attitude is the filter, or lens, through which you view your life.

We can sometimes get so caught up in blaming our situations, environment, circumstances, and people that we put our beliefs and attitudes on autopilot. When our minds are left alone, they tend to dwell on the negative aspects. We can give great excuses for the things that go wrong in our lives:

- I was raised in a poor family...
- I didn't have the opportunities others had, so I had to...
- My boss isn't nice to me, so I...
- My spouse does this, which makes me do this...
- I have to go to this training...
- It's because...
- I am doing the best I can...
- It's just not fair...
- It's not my fault...
- He/She made me....

You and I have to be in control of our "self-talk," what we say to ourselves consciously and subconsciously. We can purposefully direct the perceptions and thoughts that govern our lives.

We know people who automatically assign themselves the worst lot in life. When you ask how they are doing, they launch into an "organ recital": the dysfunctions of their liver, kidneys, stomach, and more. They're "doing okay under

49

the circumstances." Don't you ever want to ask them, "What are you doing *under* those circumstances? Get out from there!"

Have you thought of yourself as a victim in the past? Victims are helpless; they literally can't help themselves. Unless we pay attention, we, too, can become "victims" of our attitudes.

In *Learned Optimism,* Dr. Martin Seligman tells us that an epidemic has hit this country, killing more people every year than the AIDS virus. It's suicide, resulting from helpless, hopeless depression, and it's caused by the way we explain things to ourselves. Most people feel stuck. "Stuck" is two or fewer options that aren't appealing—for instance, you either go to jail or die. I don't know about you, but that would be "stuck" for me! In mental terms, if a person's future and present are the same, there is no hope, so they become helpless and hopeless. People feel there is nothing for them to live *for*—nothing to live *toward*.

It's not my intention for this chapter to become a devotional, but I often look to the *Bible* as I reset my direction. The entire book of *Ecclesiastes* deals with the reality of living without direction, and *Proverbs 13:12* acknowledges that "hope deferred makes the heart sick...." I am often encouraged by *Jeremiah 29:11:* "'For I know the plans I have for you,' declares the LORD, 'plans to prosper you and not to harm you, plans to give you hope and a future.'" The end of "hope deferred makes the heart sick" reminds me that "...a longing fulfilled is a tree of life." It assures me that my life and my goals do matter.

The blame game

When we blame other things or other people for challenges we face in life, at least two things happen:

First, we lose control. We are at the mercy of people or things that may or may not happen to us.

Second, we have a pity party for ourselves and get emotionally worked up. We allow ourselves to be "emotionally hijacked."

One of my favorite "success" posters shows a sailboat on choppy waters. The caption says, "You can't control the wind, but you can adjust your sails."

We can't control everything that happens to us in this life, but we can choose how we respond to it. Your first step is to recognize that you truly are in control of how you respond. You determine how you "replay" and "reframe" situations in your mind.

You'll recall how Nelson Mandella went from

a prison dungeon to the president's residence in South Africa. It would have been easy to become bitter, but Mandella decided to become better instead. Today, he is often associated with these words, written by Marianne Williamson:

> *Our deepest fear is not that we are inadequate. Our deepest fear is that we are powerful beyond measure. It is our light, not our darkness, that most frightens us.*

> *We ask ourselves, who am I to be brilliant, gorgeous, talented, and fabulous? Actually, who are you not to be? You are a child of God. Your playing small doesn't serve the world. There is nothing enlightened about shrinking so that other people won't feel insecure around you.*

> *We are born to make manifest the Glory of God that is within us. It's not just in some of us; it's in everyone, and as we let our own light shine, we consciously give other people permission to do the same. As we are liberated from our own fear, our presence automatically liberates others.*

We can begin becoming liberated from our fears, and creating and recognizing our inner greatness in thoughts and actions, as we evaluate the results of our old belief systems.

CHAPTER 2: **CREATE IT!**

Some of us are listening to a scratched CD that plays only, *Good nuff to get by...good nuff for tenure...good nuff for government work. Good nuff* should never be acceptable in our lives! Don't you deserve more? Don't your friends, co-workers, neighbors, employer, and family deserve better? Remember, when you live your life like it matters, it does!

If we constantly tell ourselves, "I've *never* been good at..." or "I am not a..." or "I can't...," we continue on the same dead-end path.

But we can acknowledge our faulty past views and reframe those unproductive thoughts and words. From this point on, take control of your past with this phrase: "Up until now...."

- *"Up until now,* I haven't been good at...*but now I am...."*
- *"Up until now,* I haven't been a...*but now I will...."*
- *"Up until now,* I couldn't...*but now I'm getting better...."*

What a difference when we accept responsibility for the past and give ourselves permission to move forward and create a better future!

- *"Up until now,* I haven't been good at staying in shape...*but now...."*
- *"Up until now,* I have not been a good listener...*but now...."*

- *"Up until now, I have not committed to be a better father...but now...."*
- *"But now...."*

Creating it must happen not only in our actions but in the *origins* of our thoughts and words as well. Again, it's one of those pesky, immutable, inviolable, eternal, universal laws.

Attitudes of gratitude

More than just accepting their past so they can exercise more control of their future, people who lead truly powerful lives have come to terms with the events and results of their history. They have learned to see value even in the personal failures that have shaped their lives.

Your own attitude about your past and your future controls so much of your present life. You have a captive audience who is always listening—yourself!

True success occurs when you choose to resourcefully live your life, rather than just responding to it as things happen to you. Abraham Lincoln once said, "I am not concerned that you have fallen down or get knocked down; I am concerned that you arise."

Life is about balance, and learning from the past can create a strong foundation for success. You'll find valuable information in the past, but don't live there. Focus on the future and move in the direction you are looking. Live in the now!

Let me give you a real-life example to illustrate how this approach looks—one man's past failures and how they became fuel for his future. If you've heard it before, listen with new ears and read it with new eyes. This man:

- Failed in business in '31.
- Was defeated for the Legislature in '32.
- Failed again in business in '33.
- Was elected to the Legislature in '34.
- Suffered a nervous breakdown in '36.
- Was defeated for Speaker of the Legislature in '38.
- Was defeated for Presidential elector in '40.
- Lost the Congressional nomination in '43.
- Won the Congressional election in '46.
- Was defeated for Congress in '48.
- Lost a child in '50.
- Was defeated for the U.S. Senate in '55.
- Was defeated for Vice President in '56.
- Was defeated for U.S. Senate again in '59.

Most people would have become bitter and angry at the unfairness of life. Yet, he didn't give up, asking only, "What's the use? Why keep doing this over and over again?"

NOTES TO MYSELF

BECOMING YOUR DREAMS

NOTES TO
MYSELF

He knew what he wanted. He was going to live his life like it mattered. He kept moving in the direction of his dreams...and achieved them!

I believe it was also because he understood something about destiny. He chose a different attitude, and it empowered a different response, creating a different result. The man, of course, was Abraham Lincoln. Elected President in 1860, he freed the slaves and preserved the Union through the bloody conflict of the Civil War. Nearly 150 years later, he is still viewed as one of the greatest leaders ever to occupy the White House.

What, *up until now,* has convinced you that it's a waste of your time to *Want It* and *Create It?*

Dr. Victor Frankl experienced the loss of everything you and I would think of as "necessary" to our lives in World War II's Auschwitz death camp. In writing about his life, Frankl credited his survival to one thing: "Everything can be taken from man except the last of the human freedoms: his ability to choose his own attitude in any given set of circumstances, to choose his own way."

As a speaker and consultant, I have had opportunities to meet many now-successful people who publicly share their stories of suffering and inhumanity. They, and perhaps *you,* have been abused, neglected and subjected to atrocities I don't even want to consider in this book.

What happened to them, and perhaps *you,* was wrong, unfair and disgusting. Man's inhumanity to man is well documented. It wouldn't be "wrong" for them, and perhaps *you,* to focus on all the unfairness, pain and misery in life. You could be factually correct, but what has that gotten you...*up until now?*

I have a question for them, and perhaps *you:* What do you want?

- You have been abused—*what do you want?*
- Your ex-spouse did awful things to you—*what do you want?*
- You say you weren't given opportunities that others were—*what do you want?*

Do you want to be *right,* or do you want to live a life that honors who you are and what you do? Do you want to be right, or do you want to be happy? People live in cesspools of bitterness, whether they are right or not.

Chris likes to quote Buddy Hackett, who said, "Never carry a grudge. While you are, the other guy's out dancin'." In other words, as horrible as they are—*because* of how horrible they are—get out from under your circumstances!

When you live your life in memories, you live out your history—what *once was*. When you live your life out of your imagination, you live out of all the potential you have—what *can be*. To have a new future, *Create It!*

Powerless words

Would you pour water into your gas tank? Would you put rice in your radiator? If not, why would you do the same things with your words?

Are you aware that the Bible says God simply spoke it, and there was light *(Genesis 1:3)?* There is tremendous creative power in words, even ours, so it is really important that your own *Create It* processes eliminate words that have no strength.

We use a demonstration in our seminars that proves the force of powerful, committed words and the weakening effect of powerless, uncommitted words.

Student *A* extends an arm in front of their body, parallel to the floor. *A* makes a tight fist and resists the efforts of student *B* to push down the extended arm. This is not a wrestling contest. *B* just wants to see how strong *A* is, gently pushing down with consistent, firm pressure. Depending on the relative strength of the participants, it may not require much effort from *B* to push down *A's* arm.

Then we have *A* physically resist while adding verbal commitment. When *A* says, "I *will* resist. I *will* resist. I *will* resist. I *will* resist. I *will* resist," most of our *B* students find it harder to push down *A's* much stronger arm. This is because *A* has *committed* to resist, and words and actions are congruent, so they accomplish a better result.

When we alter *A's* commitment again, with a little word, the situation is reversed dramatically. We do everything the same, except now *A* says, "I will *try* to resist." Almost all resistance fails. *A's* arm becomes noticeably weaker. *B* is often able to push *A's* arm down with only one finger. Participants are amazed!

Our words program us. What powerless words have found their way into your vocabulary? Are you using language that speaks of commitment or only of limited effort?

For instance, do you say, "I'll try to call you this afternoon?" What mental picture does this create in your head right now? I see you with Vaseline all over your hands, the phone constantly slipping from your grip. I'd rather hear that you called but couldn't reach me.

My daughter Faith told me she didn't like watching *Barney* because he says "bad words." Even a six-year-old can understand that "try" is a four-letter word! In the words of the famous philosopher, Yoda, "Do or do not; there is no *try*."

When you invite people to a meeting and they say, "I'll *try* to make it," don't save them a seat. There is no commitment in *try*. Instead, your unconscious mind realizes that you left an escape door open. There is always a possibility of, and allowance for, failure.

In our seminars, I sometimes say that the number one cause of divorce is marriage. Those who haven't experienced the pain of separation laugh, but those who have lived through the anguish understand its deep truth. In today's culture, "I do" means "I'll try." It means, "I'll give it a test drive and see how it works out."

But *try* is not true commitment. Our seminars succeed because they provide students with the experience of 100% commitment. We don't ask for 110%—that's a myth. We don't accept 85% either. All we ask, at any given time, is all you've got.

If "commit" means only *try* and not *will* to you, where else are you holding back from people who need you to step over the line and give 100%...Heart, Body and Soul?

"The future has always looked bleak, until people
with brains and faith and courage dreamed and dared
to take risks, and found a way to make it better.
If we're free to dare—and we are—if we're free to
give—and we are—then we're free to shape the
future and have within our grasp all we
dream that future will be."

— Ronald Reagan

CHAPTER 3:
LIVE IT!

Do you only *talk* your talk, or do you really *walk* your talk? Are you just saying that you *Want It*, or are you doing what's necessary to *Create It?* If you truly are committed to *becoming* the dreams of your life, you'll also need to know how to *Live It*.

Our company's purpose statement includes this definition of *Live It:* We are making the world a bit better as we live our lives with a noble cause. In other words, tomorrow is becoming better because we are here today!

Remember, when you live your life like it matters, it does. So, *Live It* is about intentional living, or living on purpose, with a mission and vision in mind.

Live it daily

John Lennon is credited with saying, "Life is what happens to you while you're busy making other plans." There's enough "same-old-same-old" in our daily lives to make us forget that history is being written as we live it every day. It's the "daily-ness" of living that causes us to lose focus on what we *want,* how we will *Create It,* and why we will *Live It.*

The plain truth is, as human development expert Bob Moawad observed, "You can't leave footprint in the sands of time if you are sitting on your butt...and who wants to leave butt prints in the sands of time?" So our focus in this chapter is how to *live* our dreams. Without this third step, we stop short of the goal.

Rather than simply challenging you to *Live It,* I challenge you to *lead it!* If you're not leading your own life, you're following someone else.

The time is now

In order to develop a sense of urgency, Empower U classes have a custom you're free to adopt. When someone asks what time it is, we reply, "The time is now...2:30" (the actual time of day). To remind ourselves that the clock is running and we must live in the present to be in control of our lives and opportunities, we precede the time by saying, "The time is now...."

We can't change the past; it has already happened. We can't control the future; it has yet to take place. The one opportunity we have to change is in this moment...*now!*

"Time is money" takes on new meaning when you remember that the Bank of Time credits you with 86,400 seconds every morning. If you think of those seconds as dollars, you'll hate wasting any of them. Every night, the Bank of Time writes off, as lost, whatever you have failed to spend wisely. The unused balance never carries over to tomorrow, there is never an overdraft. Each day, the Bank of Time credits a new 86,400 seconds to your account and burns the remainder at the end of the day. If you fail to use the day's deposits, the loss is yours. There is no going back. There is no drawing against "tomorrow." You and I must live in the present, on today's deposits. Invest your time for the greatest return in health, happiness, and success! The clock is running. *The time is now!*

To realize the value of:

one year, ask the student who failed a grade;

one month, ask the mother of a premature baby;

one week, ask the editor of a weekly newspaper;

one hour, ask the lovers who are waiting to meet;

one minute, ask the person who missed the train;

one second, ask someone who avoided an accident;

one millisecond, ask the athlete who won the *silver* medal.

Remember, time waits for no one.

NOTES TO MYSELF

EXERCISE #2

Since this is a book about becoming the leader of your life, let's look at how you are *leading* the dream you want to live. Think about where you are now and where you want to be.

It's the same drill as in Chapter 1: When you look at the following page, you'll be tempted to skip over it, since your first goal was to read this book, not to complete written assignments. But remember: How you handle the challenges in this book is a metaphor for how you handle other aspects of your life. If you shortchange *this* process, what other opportunities in your life are you shortchanging?

I challenge you to respect yourself and the process I'm trusting you to complete. Give yourself a chance to make a change—to make a difference. Here are your first two questions:

1. ***What qualities do I want to have in my life?*** (Perhaps honesty, integrity, enthusiasm, etc.)

2. ***How am I reinforcing these values?*** (If you are not, how will you do so from this point on?)

You may write your answers either on the chart or in your notebook. Don't worry about anyone else reading it. This is for *you,* and it's an opportunity to be honest with yourself.

WHAT I VALUE:	WAYS I REINFORCE THIS VALUE:									

If you've skipped this process, **STOP HERE!** No one can force you to complete the chart, but it will be worth doing so. In *Leadership Awakening,* everyone does it together, and no one moves on until all of us have finished. As a reader, *you* don't have this advantage, so you'll have to rely on *yourself* for motivation to do it. This process won't work for you if you fail yourself. Choose to pass instead.

First, on the previous page or in your notebook, write down what you value in your life or work—characteristics, qualities, or traits that are important to you. Second, write down all the ways you are reinforcing what is important to you.

In other words, do you *Want It?* What are you doing to *Create It?* In what practical ways do you *Live It?* Go ahead. Take a couple of minutes and write down what really matters to you.

Next, let's look at Questions 3 and 4:

3. ***From which roles in my life do I find the most personal satisfaction?*** (You wear a lot of "hats" in your life—which ones fit the best? The roles you enjoy may be as a spouse, a friend, a confidant, a leader or manager, a parent or coach, a sales manager or teacher. So your question is, "Where do I shine? Where do I find satisfaction?")

ROLES I ENJOY IN MY LIFE:

WHAT I LIKE MOST ABOUT MY WORK:

BECOMING YOUR DREAMS

4. ***What do I like most about the work I do?*** (Many of us tend to focus on what we don't like. So, in addition to answering *WHAT* you like about your work, also answer *WHY* you enjoy that part.)

Turn back the page and answer these two questions now.

Next, we're going to look at the "golden gripes"—issues that take away your passion and enthusiasm for the work you do. Answer these two questions:

5. ***What do I like least about my work?*** It could be your work environment, the way tasks are assigned, how people are valued, the length of your commute to your job. Whatever you put on your list, it's probably draining your energy. It's good to identify it, not as an excuse for poor performance, but to understand where you are in life.

6. ***How can I change the things I like least?*** What are two or three things you can do to lead yourself in the direction of your dreams? How can you improve your circumstances or "walk the talk" in your present situation? Rather than being the hound dog lying on a nail, what can you do to affect your outcome? Answer now.

HOW I CAN CHANGE IT:

WHAT I LIKE LEAST:

BECOMING YOUR DREAMS

You're almost finished with the Leadership Inventory. These questions—and your answers—are important considerations. We've said that you need a map for your journey, but it's important to find the **X** on the map (the "You Are Here" spot) so you'll know which direction to go.

There are 11 questions in all to answer in your Leadership Inventory. As you begin Question 7 on the next page, you're significantly more than halfway through because of the foundation you created in your first 6 answers. So press on and finish the rest!

---

7. ***What are my business' visible beliefs?*** Think about slogans, posters, charts, or a mission statement that is posted where people can see it. What does your business say it wants employees to believe?

8. ***What would be the ideal culture for my business?*** If you could wave a magic wand and create the perfect business atmosphere, what would it look like, sound like, and feel like?

9. ***How does the current business culture compare to my ideal culture?*** In essence, what's good and what needs improvement in the way your work is done? How does what exists now differ from your ideal? Where do you "walk it" and where do you only "talk it"?

VISIBLE BUSINESS BELIEFS

MY IDEAL BUSINESS CULTURE

PRESENT BUSINESS CULTURE

Now, complete Questions 7, 8, and 9 on the previous page, focusing on where you are and where you would like to be.

There are 11 questions in the Leadership Inventory, but we're saving the last two for another chapter that will focus on applying your leadership skills. As you consider your answers to the previous questions—and continue to think about them over the next few days—you'll see that you have potential to influence your work in ways you may never have considered. You have identified areas in which you can make a difference! Knowing you can is a big part of *living* your dreams.

Patterns in life

There are people who like to solve puzzles and others who think such games are a waste of time.

Cracker Barrel restaurants put a puzzle on every table for the enjoyment or frustration of their guests—have you seen it? It's a triangle-shaped piece of wood with holes drilled in it and golf tees arranged in all the holes except one. The idea is to jump pegs in checkerboard fashion, and in a straight line until you are left with only one tee.

CHAPTER 3: **LIVE IT!**

Some people who win the game occasionally and accidentally seem to enjoy the suspense as they play, wondering if, this time, they'll solve the puzzle or be left with scattered, "orphan" tees at opposite points of the triangle. There are others who win consistently because they have recognized a pattern. There are patterns in your life that determine how well you *Live It!*

I bought my son Christian a toy train big enough for him to ride on and play engineer. He was only 2½, too young to really steer it, but he thought it was fun to hold down the button on the battery-driven motor so he could ride around on the figure-8 track. He thought he was in charge, he'd found his groove. You and I know it was just a rut! The train followed a predetermined pattern. He wasn't the driver, just a passenger on a thoughtless machine.

At age 6, his sister Faith figured out that the train didn't need a track in order to work. She pulled the train off the track and chased me down the hallway with it! Faith grasped something Christian, and many adults, either don't know or won't admit: *we can change our path!* We don't have to follow that going-nowhere pattern. We can get off that track, or we can rearrange it so we go somewhere worth going.

Have you fallen into a pattern that's keeping you from living your dreams? Have you ever left work and driven home on autopilot? Arrived home without consciously thinking about the stops and turns you made? Your mind was preoccupied with other thoughts: what you did today, what you'll do tomorrow, why you're going home now, why you didn't go home sooner. Recognize your pattern. Does it at all resemble my son's figure-8 train track?

Without insights like those provided by *Leadership Awakening* and this book, some people could never leave the track. Coupled securely one to the other, it never occurs to them to do more than roll along a predetermined route to a predetermined destination.

Without a prescribed path to run on, they would quickly derail their lives. Their education and worldview has not equipped them to run off-road. My job is to show them highways—I get to explain *options!*

My daughter Faith looked at the train and where it was headed, and she saw options. You have options too. Based on what? On *what you want*. Is the track you are on leading you in circles or to your heart's destination?

Maybe your job is fine—that's not the problem. Something else is causing you to live your life at less than its passionate potential. Inside each of us is "The Little Engine That Could," and when it comes to leading the full, productive, rewarding, and happy life of your dreams, that little engine is saying, *"I think I can... I think I can... I think I can..."* Yes, you can, but will you?

Who could you have been?

I'm told that George Bernard Shaw was once asked, if he had the opportunity to go back in time and live the life of any famous and admired person in history, who would he want to be? The elderly playwright replied, "I would be the George Bernard Shaw I could have been."

By this, he meant he would live with all his potential, using all his gifts and not missing the mark. He would live without the fears of limiting belief systems that hinder our becoming who we were meant to be.

Whom do you most admire? Is it a politician, a business leader, a celebrity, an athlete, a parent, a hero? Whom do you most wish to be like? Why not be you—the *real deal*—rather than a pale imitation of someone else? You are here on this planet, at this time in history, with talent and time to truly make a difference! Be the person you could have been, and you *will be*.

Our culture loves to be graded on the curve.

Do you remember this practice from high school? Some teachers were a soft touch, and in order to determine your grade on a test, they took the highest score and counted it as perfect. Then they prorated every other student's score accordingly, raising everybody's grade.

The problem is that this practice didn't prepare you for real success in life. It taught you that *good nuff* is enough. Remember *good nuff?*

Good nuff that your spouse won't leave.

Good nuff that you won't get fired.

Good nuff for government work — ouch!

The *good nuff* scale compares you to others but never to your true self. In the *Leadership Experience* (the complete *Leadership Awakening* and *Leadership Adventure*), we never compare one participant to another. We compare the individual only with his or her own potential.

What's your sign?

In the 1970s, everybody was into astrological signs. For instance, someone might say, "I am a Libra, and my sign means I am a balanced person." One of the pickup lines at bars and night clubs of that era is still joked about today: "Hey, baby, what's your sign?"

What would your answer be? Some who study the Zodiac believe our future is locked

into the astrological sign we were assigned by
the moment of our birth. Fatalism rules over us
when we believe the die is cast and we simply
play out what has been predetermined.

Maybe your sign is "Do Not Disturb," or
"Keep Out." Do you value your individuality so
much that you exclude people? Do you value
your security so much that you exclude possibilities? Has your sign been "Yield," as you've
followed other people's plans and directions
throughout your life? Have you been unable,
until now, to focus on what really matters in
your life? If so, your sign may be "Detour." If
you've been *wanting* it but never taking the steps
to *create* it, maybe it's been a "Dead End" sign.

As of today, that's in the past. If you want
to become a leader and make a real difference—
if your drive is to be among the best of the
best—then you need a new sign: "Under Construction." Your new sign means that, like
George Bernard Shaw, you are always working
to become the you that you *could* be. Never
accepting *good nuff* from yourself or from those
around you. On a journey of continual improvement—better today than yesterday, better
tomorrow than today. As golf legend Arnold
Palmer said, "The road to success is always
'Under Construction."'

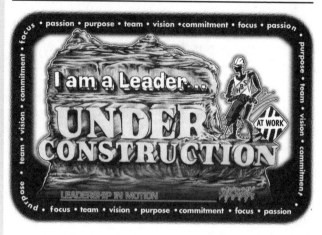

People "Under Construction" are working to improve who they are and what they do. We find them at Empower U training classes. "Under Construction" people read books and listen to audio tapes, not for entertainment but for education and self-improvement. "Under Construction" people are not looking to be comfortable, to get by with *good nuff*. They are looking to excel, to have an impact, to make a difference.

Take the dare

How do you get onto your "Under Construction" journey? There are times when you begin by choice. You see that there are options in life. You believe you were made for more than what you have. You decide it's time to go for it.

Other times, it is...just...time. Circumstances align when opportunity and preparedness meet.

You've studied and prepared yourself, and your time has arrived. Your time can be *now!*

Sometimes life thrusts us into incredible opportunities for growth, providing optimal chances to really learn who we are and what we are made of. These are times we most want to avoid (as we are experiencing them) and cherish most when they are over and we have learned a life lesson.

It is in these times that "major construction" can take place, if we choose. The loss of a job or spouse, a transfer, a medical condition, being ostracized from an organization you helped build—whatever the circumstance—you find that you are "Under Construction." At the moment, it may feel like the demolition is tearing away your foundations. There is nothing in you that believes you can ever *Live It*. At best, you hope you can just *survive it*.

Life has hurled a challenge at you, and you're discovering that there is a price to be paid in pursuing your prize. My writing partner Chris wrote a book called *The Price and the Prize,* in which he identified three things that are always true of the price you will pay for your success:

1. ***Your price will always be personal.*** After all, no one wants "generic" success. You want personal success that means some-

thing to you. Expect your personal prize to have a personal price.

2. ***Your price will always be costly.*** Value always demands a high price, and often, money alone will not meet the cost. You must invest yourself, your energies, and your best.

3. ***The price is never negotiable.*** The cost of success must always be paid in full. When we try to shortcut it, we shortchange our results.

So it's important that the personal, costly, never-negotiable price we pay is worth the prize we are pursuing. Many times, this price causes people to stop at the *Want It* phase. After all, it costs very little to be a *wannabe*. Others find the resources to push past *Want It* into *Create It* and see their dream take shape. But they may hold back from taking possession of their dreams because *Live It* requires more challenge, commitment, and sacrifice.

If you are undergoing the tests of "major construction," keep in mind that you don't know how close you are to emerging from the thick forest described in Chapter 2. You are pursuing a prize of great value. Soon, if you continue to pursue it, you will *become* your dreams.

CHAPTER 3: LIVE IT!

You've heard the saying, "What you do speaks louder than what you say." As you complete this book and accomplish your dreams, people are watching you. Instead of telling people what you're going to do, show them. Let your actions speak louder than your words.

The Time Is Now...to *Live It!*

NOTES TO MYSELF

Congratulations! By completing the work assignments in these first three chapters, you have established a solid foundation for what follows. The next six chapters will provide you with tools to help you build your dream life of success, meaning, and fulfillment. You are becoming your dreams!

BECOMING YOUR DREAMS

SECTION II: YOUR 6-PIECE TOOL BOX

"It is not the critic who counts; not the man who points out how the strong man stumbled, or where the doer of deeds could have done them better. The credit belongs to the man who is actually in the arena; whose face is marred by dust and sweat and blood; who strives valiantly; who errs and comes short again and again; who knows the great enthusiasms, the great devotions, and spends himself in a worthy cause; who at the best knows in the end the triumph of high achievement; and who at the worst, if he fails, at least fails while daring greatly; so that his place shall never be with those cold and timid souls who know neither victory nor defeat."

— Theodore Roosevelt

CHAPTER 4:
PASSION!

NOTES TO
MYSELF

pas-sion \păsh'-ən\ *n* 1: a powerful emotion, such as love, joy, hatred, or anger. 2: ardent love. 3: boundless enthusiasm 4: an abandoned display of emotion.

My personal rallying cry is "Passion—Heart, Body and Soul." It declares that I live my life with everything I've got. All of my will, strength, courage, boldness, effort, emotion, enthusiasm, determination, drive, desire, devotion, thoughts, actions, love, motivation—every bit focused on the worthiness of reaching my goals and being my dreams. I have a passion so all-encompassing that its powerful energy makes it possible for me to *Want It, Create It, Live It* in my life. Passion can do the same for you!

On a crusade

You may not know the name Guy Kawasaki *(hint:* he did not invent the motorcycle!), so I'll tell you that he, with partners Steve Wozniak and Steve Jobs, founded a company called Apple. They were empowered by their Passion to harness the potential of the personal computer for people like you and me. So strong was their commitment to this quest that they became known as "Mac evangelists." Their missionary zeal to spread the "good news" about personal computing was, to many, fanatical.

In his book, *Selling the Dream,* Kawasaki explained the power of Passion in creating success:

"To the luckiest of people, a time comes when they join or launch a cause that forever changes their lives and the lives of others. Losing yourself in a cause is delicious and intoxicating; the best word to describe the sensation is 'crusade.'

"The first thing you need to believe about a crusade is *never underestimate its power.* It can transform ordinary people, products, and companies into devastating flamethrowers!

"You have to have a *passionate* desire to make a difference and fearlessly believe in your cause."

Passion fueled everything in the early days of Apple Computer. It probably even got in the way at times, given the fiery tempers and fierce dedication of the company's founders. As the company grew, president Steve Jobs knew they needed more business skills than they possessed.

So they searched for a world-class executive who could lead the company. Eventually, Jobs was led to John Scully, then president of PepsiCo. In what is now a legendary conversation, Scully asked Jobs why he should even consider leaving Pepsi when it was expanding into China and he was heading up successful enterprises like Taco Bell, Pizza Hut, Kentucky Fried Chicken, and more. Jobs, passionate about his crusade, replied, "Do you want to sell sugar water the rest of your life, or do you want to change the world?"

Passion won out, and Apple won a new CEO.

Understanding passion

Passion is, at its base, about having strong feelings. The Greek meaning for the word is emotion—the indispensable fuel that propels us to greatness. Everything important that happens to us arouses our emotions.

Many people believe that emotions have no place in the workplace, that emotions and business do not mix. This archaic way of thinking harms the life-force of an enterprise, as well as the people who make up the organization.

When many people think of emotions, they visualize someone weakly sitting and weeping—that's not what I mean. Others think of emotions as wild demonstrations of anger. The modern translation of Aristotle's 350 BC *Nicomachean Ethics* says, "Anyone can become angry; that's easy. But to be angry with the right person, to the right degree, at the right time, for the right purpose, and in the right way—this is not easy."

As I've asked leaders and managers from all over the world what they consider to be the greatest leadership qualities, these powerful, one-word responses have stood out repeatedly:

- Enthusiastic
- Inspirational
- Empathetic
- Caring
- Passionate
- Charismatic
- Compassionate
- Exciting

All of these are emotional words, but they are just words unless energy and Passion back them up and bring them to life!

Most people have to become angry to tap into Passion. When thought of in that sense, Passion becomes a negative force for them and those around them. Passion was present in Kosovo and in the Nazi death camps during Hitler's reign. Corrupted passion brought down the World Trade Center.

Some people only experience Passion inside the bedroom, where passionate words may be spoken behind closed doors. Because of this, they believe Passion only takes place in intimate settings between two people.

Sure, Passion may be present in these situations, but it's much more than tyrannical destruction of people and things or a private connection between individuals. Passion is what makes achievers get up each day, do what they do with excellence, and do it again...and again...and again until they achieve their dreams.

Passion is emotion, intense emotion! Emotions are neither *good* nor *bad*—it's what we do with our emotions that puts value on them. When we learn that, we can tap into an energy source with as much power, in a positive way, as splitting atoms! The more we learn to understand and direct our emotions, the better we can serve our world and truly make a difference.

Developing emotional intelligence

Today's leaders understand that it's important to develop *emotional intelligence, or EQ,* so we know ourselves, our strengths and limitations, our insights and blind spots. Then we can harness the tremendous power of Passion inside us. Then we can effectively inspire and motivate others to our cause. In his book, *Executive EQ: Emotional Intelligence in Leadership and Organizations,* Dr. Robert Cooper defines emotional intelligence as the "ability to sense, understand, and effectively apply the power and acumen of emotions as a source of human energy, information, connection and influence."

It's not enough to have feelings. Emotional intelligence requires that we learn to acknowledge and value these feelings—in ourselves and others—and that we respond appropriately to them, effectively applying the information and energy in our daily life and work. Your EQ is a better barometer for success than your IQ.

Joshua Hammond, president of American Quality Foundation, says understanding and using the strength of our emotions is a key factor in every leading enterprise, but it is unrecognized and unvalued by most of today's business organizations. New studies suggest that in most cases, *too little* emotion is at least as devastating to a career or organization as *too much* emotion.

Recently, as a result of such studies, a major shift has occurred in the way many people look at the usefulness of emotion in business and leadership. Companies like Coca-Cola, Cintas, Baylor Medical Center Foundation, and Avail Medical send their leaders to Empower U so their executives will get "fired up" and raise the bar. Admittedly, not everyone is happy with, or agreeable to, this modern view, but when our emotions serve us intelligently, amazing results are reported. The following chart compares old and new views on the subject:

CONVENTIONAL	HIGH-PERFORMANCE
Emotions distract us	Emotions motivate us
Sign of weakness	Sign of strength
No place in business	Crucial in business
Good manager	Powerful leader
Makes us vulnerable	Makes us real, alive
Avoid emotions	Emotions trigger learning
Controlling	Empowering
Get rid of them	Integrate them
Avoid emotional words	Use emotional words
Suspicious	Informed
Interferes with business	Drives the mission

If I were to ask you what you believe are the greatest assets in your company, what would you answer? Not your buildings or land, not your computers or databases. Not even trademarks or copyrights. I believe the greatest asset of any company is the hearts and minds of its people.

Companies do many things to train the minds of their managers and employees, but traditional business has long neglected issues of the heart. We're starting to see a different approach as forward-thinking managers tap into the heart motivations of their employees.

BECOMING YOUR DREAMS

Is your workplace on fire with Passion? Do those around you bring their hearts to work? The heart is the place of courage, spirit, integrity, commitment, compassion, empathy, understanding, caring, and many other leadership characteristics. It is a source of energy that calls us to learn, cooperate, lead, and serve.

Recent bestselling books, such as *Becoming a Person of Influence, Who Moved My Cheese?,* and *Fish!,* are reminders that it's easier to *encourage cooperation* than *enforce compliance* when leading people. We lead best from an intelligent heart—one that *thinks* and *feels.*

Peter Senge, author of *The Fifth Discipline* and former Director of the Organizational Learning Center at Massachusetts Institute of Technology (MIT) stated it best when he said: "People with high levels of personal mastery...cannot afford to choose between reason and intuition, or the head and the heart, any more than they would choose to walk on one leg or see with one eye."

Emotions come from the heart, where our deepest values are activated. The heart knows things the mind does not and cannot. Blaise Pascal, a great physicist and philosopher, observed, "The heart has its reasons, which reason cannot understand."

CHAPTER 4: **PASSION!**

To quote Dr. Robert Cooper again: "By and large, what we are searching for in business and in life isn't *out there,* in the latest trends or technology; it's *in here,* inside ourselves. It has been there all along, but we have not valued it, or respected it, or used it as brilliantly as we are capable of. At its essence, a meaningful and successful life requires being *attuned to what is on the inside,* beneath the mental analyses, the appearances and control, beneath the rhetoric and skin. In the human heart."

What is emotional intelligence, and where does it come from? It's not pretending that you're happy; it's not acting as if you have no emotions, or suppressing your emotions until you explode. Emotional intelligence is intelligent use of the heart's information—having the right emotion, the right intensity, at the right time, directed at the right person for the right purpose. This is not easy!

As Dr. Cooper points out, EQ comes not from the musings of some rarified intellect, but from the workings of the human heart. Emotional intelligence allows us to understand and pursue our unique potential and purpose, and it activates our innermost values and aspirations, transforming them from *things we think about* to *what we live.*

95

BECOMING YOUR DREAMS

If you have a word processor, would you want employees using a typewriter? If you have two good legs, would you hop on only one? If you have a chain saw, would you use a hand saw to chop down a tree? No, you'd use the best you have to get the best results. So why not inspire and encourage your business team to use the best they have—including the power of their emotions—to accomplish their purpose?

Become a passionate leader

Leadership is *action,* not position. Being a leader is about being a role model. You can't expect your team members to be excited and emotionally involved with your mission and purpose if you, a leader, are not. Enthusiasm and Passion are contagious. When you are enthusiastic and passionate about what you are doing, people around you usually become more enthusiastic and passionate about what they are doing with you. (We'll discuss this in greater depth in Chapter 7, considering the value of Team.)

Passion is one of a leader's greatest qualities. People want to be around passionate individuals; they are looking for passion in their own lives. We all have internal flames of passion burning within, but sometimes we let circumstances or situations douse that flame. People lose or switch jobs, marriages dissolve, children get sick, planes crash and people die, and sometimes our passion wanes. Our internal candle is extinguished. To re-ignite that flame or to make it burn brighter, ask yourself:

- In what ways do I make a difference?
- Why am I here?
- In what activities do I feel most fulfilled?
- What is my unique purpose in life?

As you answer these questions, dig down deep—and feel your flame grow hotter.

People want to know that they are important—even *necessary*—and a part of something bigger than they are. When you can help them get emotionally involved with what they do, you have served your team well. To quote Clarence Francis, "You can buy a person's time; you can buy his or her physical presence at a given place; you can even buy a measured number of their skilled muscular motions per hour. But you cannot buy *enthusiasm*…you cannot buy *loyalty*. You cannot buy the *devotion* of hearts, minds, or souls. You must earn these."

An executive for Coca-Cola's Mid-Atlantic Operations once told me that Coke doesn't think of itself as being in the soft-drink business.

BECOMING YOUR DREAMS

Instead, it's a people-business that supplies soft drinks. This concept is the basis for a program Empower U has developed with Coke, called *Putting People First!*

To be a passionate leader, you must become a passionate *builder* of people and their dreams. Remember the three stonecutters who were asked to describe their task? The first said he was breaking up some rocks. The second said he was raising a wall. The third said he was building a cathedral. All three were doing the same job on the same work site, yet only one saw the real value in his efforts.

As a leader, what are you building of value? Giving only what's required in your job description is like breaking rocks. Meeting your company's expectations or reaching your stated objectives is like raising a wall. Leading people is like building a cathedral.

Passion on display

John Wesley, the evangelist and founder of Methodism, trained a group of ministers— "circuit-riding preachers"—who took to the back country on horseback, drawing crowds to hear the gospel message. But Wesley himself continued to draw much larger crowds to hear his enthusiastic calls for repentance and faith, and his students asked how they could also get throngs of people to come and listen. Wesley's advice was, "Set yourself on fire for God, and people will come for miles to watch you burn!"

Wesely's passion and enthusiasm for God sparked a worldwide revival, the effects of which are still being felt more than 300 years after his death. According to religious historians, his eloquent and vehement opposition to the slave trade led the way, 60 years after he died, to American abolition and Abraham Lincoln's *Emancipation Proclamation.*

Two old Christian songs are about burning brightly. The first says, "Let me burn out for Thee, O God." The second says, "Give me oil in my lamp, keep me burning." I don't know about you, but I prefer to burn *on* rather than burn *out. Your* passionate enthusiasm that will attract followers to watch *you* burn brightly!

While we're on the subject, did you know that the word *enthusiasm* has a religious origin? *En + theos,* literally translated as "of the spirit," describes God bubbling out from inside us. In other words, enthusiasm is Passion on display for all to see.

In his book, *Life Is Tremendous,* Charles "Tremendous" Jones, one of the great motivational writers and speakers of our time, explains that enthusiasm isn't an *act* you do but an attitude that flows up and over from inside. It can't be held down or held back.

That's true—once you get the stopper out of the bottle—but maybe your "cork" has been blocking the flow for a long time. Uncorking Passion is why, during our *Leadership Experience* seminars, we challenge participants to do everything, for 72 hours straight, with Passion...Heart, Body and Soul.

Edward B. Butler, born almost 400 years ago, understood what most of our participants discover for the first time in our *Leadership Awakening* seminar. Butler wrote, "One man has enthusiasm for 30 minutes, another for 30 days, but it is the man who has it for 30 years who makes a success of his life." It's the *habit* of passionate enthusiasm that makes a difference!

Charles Schwab said, "A man can succeed at almost anything for which he has unlimited enthusiasm."

Thomas Edison said, "When a man dies, if he can pass enthusiasm along to his children, he has left them an estate of incalculable wealth."

CHAPTER 4: PASSION!

Winston Churchill said, "Success is the ability to go from one failure to another with no loss of enthusiasm."

Another word that goes with Passion is *inspiration*. It also has theological origins. Its Greek meaning is "God-breathed," expressing that our great words, thoughts, and ideas are breathed into us by God, just as surely as our breath is.

When speaking about leadership, media mogul Ted Turner said, "Inspiration and Passion usually go together. If you're going to persuade others to go with you, it certainly doesn't hurt that you've got very strong convictions about where you are going. Like Columbus did, for instance, to discover the New World. And, if you've got Passion and conviction, you're more likely to be inspiring. If you're inspired yourself and you're passionate about something, you're more likely to succeed at it, and you're more likely to get others to come with you."

So, Passion on display—enthusiasm and inspiration—breathes life into others. When these are matched with *conviction,* the absolute certainty that what you're doing is as right as it is necessary, you'll burn so brightly that you light up the sky. And you'll light the way for others to follow.

BECOMING YOUR DREAMS

People will want to be on your team. They'll come from miles to watch you burn. With inspiration, some will catch the spark and get on fire with you!

Passion: it's what leaders have.

I am love...I am desire...
I make you toss and turn at night,
Keeping you from sleep—and yet not tired.
I am fear...I am anger...I can be rage!
You can experience me in Love,
Laughter, and Happiness...and at any age.
I was there in Auschwitz, I was there in Rome,
I was at the Sistine chapel, I am in too few a home.
It was I who sent a man to the moon.
It was I who freed the slaves.
It was I who fought the two World Wars
and buried many men in their graves!
It was because of me that Christ went to Jerusalem—
it was because of me that women finally got to vote.
It was because of me that our Founding Fathers wrote
the Constitution, and we have defended it since—
fighting battles from coast to coast.
With or without me, things will get done.
If I am not there, life can lose meaning, substance,
and purpose and be of little fun.
If you are lucky enough to possess me,
then you shall be rewarded...
For you have found PASSION—and the difference
you make will be forever recorded!

Scott V. Black

"When nothing seems to help, I go and look at a stonecutter hammering away at his rock, perhaps a hundred times without as much as a crack showing in it. Yet, at the hundred and first blow, it will split in two—and I know it was not that blow that did it but all that had gone before."

— Jacob Riis

CHAPTER 5:

FOCUS!

fo·cus \fō′-kəs\ *n* 1: a point at which rays of light or other radiation converge or from which they appear to diverge, as after refraction or reflection in an optical system. 2: the distinctness of clarity of an image rendered by an optical system. 3: a center of interest or activity. 4: close or narrow attention; concentration. 5: a condition in which something can be clearly apprehended or perceived.

When you learn something new, you begin at a stage called *unconscious incompetence.* This means you don't know what you don't know. You don't understand what's missing in your knowledge. Your teacher's task is to bring you to the next stage, *conscious incompetence.* Here, you aren't any more competent, but at least you know that you don't know—and you're more aware of what you need to learn. Your target becomes the third stage, in which you become *consciously competent.* This means you can do what you need to do, but your competence depends on total focus and concentration. Your ultimate goal is called *unconscious competence,* in which you become so good at what was once difficult that you can do it without thinking about it.

BECOMING YOUR DREAMS

The first step participants take in our *Leadership Awakening* seminar is looking at the tool of Focus, become aware of how unaware they really are.

You see, *unconscious incompetence* is a dangerous zone to operate in, where you not only don't know the truth, but you don't know that you don't know the truth. And much of what you think you do know isn't so!

Where do most of us get the idea that we really know what's going on? Maybe it happens when we graduate from high school or college and someone hands us a piece of paper that says we're educated. We think the paper tells us we're *competent,* that we know what we need for life, so we stop deliberate learning.

According to the American Booksellers Association:

- 80% of U.S. families did not buy or read a book in the past year
- 70% of U.S. adults have not been in a bookstore in the last five years
- 58% of the adult U.S. population never reads another book after high school
- 42% of college graduates never read another book after graduation

106

We're told that the quantity of available information doubles every year. Frankly, that's too much to learn! We can't know *everything*, much to the dismay of our friends who have high Theoretical values (see Chapter 1). So we need to identify our core truths and make sure we understand them well. An increased quantity of knowledge doesn't always yield increased quality.

You'll learn faster when you admit there are many things you don't know that you should know and begin your *focused* campaign to learn your core truths—what matters in your life.

Dodge the decoys

To succeed where it really counts, to extend your influence, to be an effective leader, you must Focus on what's really important. Where we tend to lose Focus is in little things that pull us off course. Chris calls these distractions decoys. In duck hunting, fake ducks can be placed in a pond or lake to lure migrating ducks down from their safe flying altitudes to within range of a hunter's shotgun. Your life and your business are full of decoys, and if you allow yourself to be distracted by them, you'll be a dead duck.

What are the decoys that lure you away

107

from being the kind of spouse, parent, leader, employee, and person you want to be?

- Are you "majoring in minors"? What really counts and deserves your Focus? What's less worthy of your time, efforts, and energies, and what's unworthy altogether?
- Are you focusing on past mistakes instead of what you can do right today that will create a better tomorrow?
- Are you focused on what you *can* do or what you *can't?* Is your Focus on your successes or your failures?
- Are you focusing on what you *don't* want, instead of what you *do* want.

Think about Harry Chapin's song, *Cat's in the Cradle,* in which a little boy's dad was too busy to watch him grow or teach him to pitch. The dad was the boy's hero, and the boy always told him, "I'm gonna be like you." As he reached his college years, the boy figured out that his dad never made time for him so he made no time for his dad. Then, as an adult, he became just like his dad. I think the son wanted so much to be *unlike* his dad that he focused on the negative—what he didn't want—until he created it in himself. It's an important lesson, because we get what we focus on; we end up where we focus.

Still another challenge for talented and skilled people is that they are in demand everywhere. It's easy to lose Focus when everyone else wants your time and you're good at almost everything you do. How do you distinguish between a decoy and an opportunity? The following exercise is designed to help you determine your Focus.

EXERCISE #3

Much like the previous exercises, there are questions for you to answer on the following pages. As before, you may feel tempted to skip them, but how you handle challenges in this book reveal how you handle other challenges in your life. Shortchanging *this* process shows how you cheat yourself of rewards in your life. Just do it!

---

1. ***What are my greatest strengths and personal talents?*** (What's *best* about you, not just *good nuff?*)

2. ***If I had unlimited time and resources, what would I choose to do?*** (Are you majoring in the majors or majoring in the minors of your life?)

Write your answers on the following chart or in your notebook. Don't worry about anyone else—this is for you. Turn the page and begin.

BECOMING YOUR DREAMS

① MY STRENGTHS AND PERSONAL TALENTS:

② WHAT I WOULD CHOOSE TO DO:

110

The question about unlimited time and resources is good, but no one has either. And we have only this life to get it right. I think your *time* is even more important to you than your *financial* resources. If I'm foolish and squander my money, I may have opportunities to regain it and maybe more. But I have no way of winning back my time—once it's lost, it's gone for good. Lord Chesterton wrote, "I recommend that you take care of the minutes, and the hours will take care of themselves." It's in our minutes that we make or break our hours, days, and years.

Answer these questions on the next page:

---

3. *When I reflect on my personal life and business, what activities do I consider of greatest value or worth?* (Where is your life invested for greatest return and satisfaction?)

4. *What are the most important relationships in my life? Why?* (How are your associations contributing to your Focus? Are you allowing yourself to be distracted by decoys? Is it possible that you are a decoy for someone else?)

Again, your answers are for you. Our intent is to help you decide where you will Focus your time, money, and energy. Write your answers now, either here or in your notebook.

---

③ **ACTIVITIES OF GREATEST VALUE:**

④ **MY MOST IMPORTANT RELATIONSHIPS:**

If your work requires dealing with people, are there times when you think it would be easier if you could do it all on your own? Yet, our value is rated according to the contributions we make to other people. (Notice I didn't say people are always compensated fairly for the value they bring to others; I said only that it's important for us to contribute and bring value.) Most of us want to make our mark in the world—so people will be glad we're here and miss us when we're gone.

Think about contributors to your life. How many mothers and fathers were you given? How many did your children get? How many first grade teachers taught you to spell and count? How many first bosses did you have on your first job? How many love interests gave you your first kiss? Each of these *individuals* made a difference in your life, and you may still feel their influence today.

So, on the following page or in your notebook, consider this question about how and when and where you spend your time and energy:

---

5. *In what ways do I make a difference?* What are *you* doing that makes it matter that you are on this planet at this time?

BECOMING YOUR DREAMS

⑤ **WAYS I MAKE A DIFFERENCE:**

114

Where to focus

The last question considered the difference one person can make. When I take people into the desert for our *Leadership Experience Part II* seminar, *Leadership Adventure,* one person's lack of Focus can be dangerous. We do tasks as teams that require constant thought and concern for each other, yet some people seem more concerned about how they *look* than how they *perform*. They put their Focus on doing things by themselves, for themselves. The way they "cover their butts" to avoid failure sometimes causes others to fail instead.

But *Adventure* can't be completed alone! Seemingly insurmountable tasks are accomplished when team members focus on helping each other. Each participant's success becomes a by-product of team success. Some people Focus on a *thing*—the certificate awarded at the end of our time in the desert, for instance— and they can actually fail to earn it. Are you focusing on people or things?

I'm constantly surprised at the number of professional speakers whose lives have defied failures, hardships, and disabilities. I become inspired and motivated to do more with my own life when I hear their stories. Their joy and fulfillment come from focusing on their achievements, not on their handicaps. As David Ring, a popular speaker afflicted with cerebral palsy, says to his audiences, "Don't whine—*shine!*" What are you focusing on?

W. Mitchell has been confined to his wheelchair since a fiery accident claimed his fingers and feet years ago. He travels the world teaching principles of achievement and success. He says, "Before I was paralyzed, there were 10,000 things I could do. Now there are 9,000. I could dwell on the 1,000 I lost or focus on the 9,000 I have left." His secret isn't just thinking positive thoughts; it's choosing where he puts his Focus. Where is yours?

The *Bible* tells us we're better off focusing on what is pure, just, honest, right, good, strong, praiseworthy *(Philippians 4:8)*. This isn't some kind of denial that ignores what's wrong. It directs attention to possibilities for progress and correction. It asks:

- What will I do?
- How will I handle this?
- How will I use this?
- How will I change this?

Asking these questions presumes one thing: *I will do something.* You and I must take action that focuses on changing our situations. Left alone, our minds tend to go toward the negative.

We must focus on where and how to respond, or else we will drift toward unproductive attitudes and results.

This is why, in some of my toughest moments, I say to myself, "This just makes a better story." I understand that the hardship I'm enduring will make my success story more interesting. But it's not denial, or pretending my circumstances aren't real or that they will go away on their own. In looking to a brighter future, I don't deny the reality of my present situation. I choose to focus on the positive.

Here's another way to look at it: Have you ever seen the bumper sticker that says, "Wherever you are, be there"? It's a cute slogan, but the truth is that wherever you *are* isn't *there*— it's *here!* By definition, *there* is somewhere else. *There* can be where you *were* or where you *will be*, but *here* is where you *are* now. Wherever you are, put your Focus *here*. What are the things you need to do *here*, whether you want to *get to there* or *get out of there?* Even in the presence of challenges, keep your Focus where it counts—be *here!*

What is the object of your Focus? What are you thinking about? John Cowper Powers said, "What we steadily, consciously, habitually think we are, that we tend to become."

117

BECOMING YOUR DREAMS

NOTES TO
MYSELF

I've heard people say if that were really true, most teenage boys would become teenage girls! But Powers didn't actually say we become what we think *about;* he said we become what we think we *are.* If we waste time focusing on a poor self-image, we become the losers we tell ourselves we are.

In effect, images in our minds become "tracks" for our behavior to follow, inevitably leading to poor self-image. Then our internal CD player kicks in, repeating the Loser's Lyrics: "What's the use, nothing matters anyway." Before we know it, we are getting exactly what we *don't* want.

Golfer Jack Nicklaus knows the things he gives attention to gain power in his life. This is why he says, "Focus on *remedies,* not faults." If he got to the tee and thought about what could go wrong in his golf swing, or the poor practice round he had previously, he wouldn't have been the peak performer he has been in his career. Rather than finding fault, he finds solutions. That's what consistent winners do.

Focus on your progress and achievements, not on your shortcomings. Scientist Marie Curie observed a truth about human nature when she wrote, "One never notices what has been done; one can only see what remains to be done."

Her statement reminds me of the saying that it's hard to remember that your original goal was to drain the swamp when you're up to your armpits in alligators! Other demands may interrupt our progress, and we can forget what we came to do. We can look at the obstacles and feel we've failed to move ahead, or we can reframe Curie's statement in our lives: *"Up until now*...I've found it easier to notice what remains to be done. *From now on,* I will also acknowledge what I've already achieved!"

Laser Focus

As a kid, did you ever get into mischief with a magnifying glass and an anthill? The sun's energy, concentrated through the lens, could crinkle those armored insects and send other ants scurrying.

In 1958, when scientists at Bell Labs were working to invent the laser—the most powerful light form on our planet, 10 times more powerful than the sun—it was first formed from a single, sharply-focused *40-watt* light bulb.

In both of these examples, the light already existed, but its power had to be contained and directed. It's the same with Focus. The energy you possess inside—the human spirit—

119

dwarfs the energy of a light bulb. But you have little power in using it if your light is diffused rather than concentrated. Imagine the power, the potential, of focusing your energy on what you want. Remember, when you live your life like it matters, it *does!*

In some of our training sessions, it's possible for students to break boards and walk across searing coals when they develop laser-like Focus. How can *you* achieve this kind of powerful Focus for *your* goals and dreams? The skill of focusing doesn't have to be a long, drawn-out process. Believe it or not, if you want to have Focus, *focus!*

You and I were born with the ability to focus. Somehow we lose much of it, perhaps from lack of use. Think about this: A newborn baby with little muscle tone grabs hold of your ear or nose and won't let go. How can such a tiny infant "lock on" with such strength? *Focus!* Yet, if someone jingles a set of keys and distracts the baby, you're immediately set free. Sometimes, I think we adults have more experience with distractions than with Focus.

If you want to be committed, make sure you *commit.* Just settle it. If you decide to *act,* to *change,* to *do,* you don't have to revisit that decision every time. In the same way, extend your commitment to focusing on what matters. Move forward with a clear Focus on what you want and how you will create it.

Persistence pays

A final thought about Focus involves sticking with it. Curtis Dahl wrote, "He had so many irons in the fire that he was never able to forge any single one into a weapon with which to conquer his world."

Could Dahl have been writing about you? A few pages ago, I mentioned people who are so good at everything they do that others continually decoy them with requests for assistance. I think Dahl was writing about a man who could have succeeded at almost anything but allowed his own *potential* to decoy him. He thought, "I could be good at this...I could be good at that...And maybe I should dabble in something else, too."

While we sometimes allow ourselves to be lose Focus because we have so many options for success, you and I can also be decoyed by our fear of failing. When the going got tough, have you ever thought it would be better for you to "broaden your Focus" and do something that seemed easier or more sure? Learn to *persist* at the tasks you commit to completing. Leaders

121

stick through the difficult struggles and that
makes them stronger.

Like the magnifying glass, the bigger the
circle of light under the glass, the less heat and
less power. Instead of widening our Focus in hope
that something might catch fire, we need to
tighten our Focus so energy is harnessed and
power is produced.

President Calvin Coolidge said, "Nothing
in the world can take the place of persistence.
Talent will not; nothing is more common than
unsuccessful men with talent. Genius will not;
unrewarded genius is almost a proverb. Education will not; the world is full of educated
derelicts. Persistence and determination alone
are omnipotent. The slogan 'Press on' has
solved, and always will solve, the problems of
the human race."

Focus: it's what leaders do.

Answer Me This

What is the message You want me to know?
What is this lesson, I need to grow?
What is the reason for the trouble and despair?
Why this relationship too ill to repair?
When will I know what You want me to do?
Where will I hear instructions from You?
Why do I need to experience this pain?
Why the need for the constant reframe?
Please answer these questions, I need to know
If I were You, this is how it would go...
The message is, "I love you," no matter the what,
Learn to hear better...works better when the mouth is shut!
Pain creates a chasm for the joy to fill up,
You went on your own; now drink of your cup.
Love others, with yourself in that group too.
My message, quite clear, you know what to do.
Your pain—quite minimal—in these minor leagues,
The joy of Me in Heaven, move beyond with intrigue.
For I am your Father, you need Me, I know
Well done with what I gave you... It's been quite a show.

Scott V. Black

"We can do whatever we wish to do provided our wish
is strong enough. What do you want most to do?
That's what I have to keep asking myself
in the face of difficulties."

— Katherine Mansfield

CHAPTER 6:
COMMITMENT!

com-mit-ment \kə-mĭt′-mənt\ *n* 1: the act or an instance of committing, especially: (a) the act of referring a legislative bill to committee. (b) official consignment, as to a prison or mental health facility. (c) a court order authorizing consignment to a prison. 2: (a) a pledge to do. (b) something pledged, especially an engagement by contract involving financial obligation. 3: the state of being bound emotionally or intellectually to a course of action or to another person or persons.

We could have begun this chapter on Commitment with the last chapter's final quote on persistence, but I think persisting has more to do with maintaining your Focus under fire than being committed.

Some people confuse *participation* for *Commitment*. A great example is the story of the chicken and the pig that are discussing world hunger. The chicken suggests they could help the hungry with a ham and egg breakfast. The pig points out that the chicken would only be a participant, but the pig would have to be totally committed!

What's the difference between giving an egg and giving your leg? The pig knew;

the chicken had no clue.

Do you know the difference between saying yes with your mouth and saying yes with your Heart, Body and Soul? With only half a smile, I tell seminar audiences that the number one cause of divorce in this country is marriage, because when people say "I *do*," many really mean "I'll *try*."

"I'll *try*" is taking a test-drive, giving it a shot, seeing what happens. But don't count on me if it doesn't work to my liking.

Your words and actions must be congruent. Commitment at the point of decision is true commitment. Remember, what you do speaks so loudly, I can't hear what you're saying.

Let me give you an example. I "decide" I'm going to get back in shape. I pack my gym bag at night so, when my alarm goes off at 4:30 in the morning, I can jump out of bed and head to the gym. I am *committed!* Then, I'm jarred from my slumber when the alarm starts ringing at that ridiculous hour, and I really could use another hour or two of sleep. My actions show whether my Commitment is real.

Try, try again

Have you ever told someone, "I tried to call you"? When I hear that, I envision you

126

duct-taped to a chair bolted to the floor. You're straining to grasp a telephone just out of reach. With all your effort, you finally grab the phone, only to discover it's been coated in oil! It slips from your hand, no matter what you do. Is this what actually happened? Of course not.

At best, when people tell me they *tried* to call, it means they *would have if*.... They didn't, because something else got in the way—something else was more important. Did they break their word to me? Maybe. Maybe not. *Try* isn't much of a promise in the first place. "I'll *try*" is the language of people who do *good nuff;* "I'll *do*" is the language of people who *win*. I *will/I will not* is the language of Commitment.

Do your words and actions match? Are you using words of Commitment when you set goals and communicate with others? With powerless words, failure is always an option. You have a built-in excuse if it doesn't work: "I told you I tried...I did my best...." Are you committed or are you still *trying?* Are you always going to have a reason why you couldn't?

Do you want to make changes in your life? Success doesn't depend on the sincerity of your desire but the intensity of your Commitment. If you don't like the results, change the approach. What do you want?

Your most important change needs to happen in your BS! I don't mean stuff you get on your shoes when walking through a pasture—I mean your Belief System. It's what your mind believes about your abilities, inabilities, disabilities, and possibilities. In the past, you've hit internal resistance, usually a belief that you're either powerless or unworthy. Often, it does its job without your noticing. What are you holding on to that is holding you back?

EXERCISE #4

No matter how well we're doing, we can do better. False beliefs pull us backward from one side while our true vision of who we can be tugs at us to move forward. What's pulling you backward? Fear of failure, rejection, or embarrassment? Self-sabotage? Past programming from someone who verbally abused you, saying you'll never amount to anything? In this exercise, you'll see 20 false beliefs. As we go through them, you'll see that many are interrelated. They are:

1. **Fear of risking.** Are you afraid to step out into the unknown? Are you stuck and stagnant, not growing?

Fear of risking can keep everything else stuck in place. There's a tale about a World War II Nazi

128

Commandant picked a POW to execute every day. He taunted his victims with the choice of a simple bullet to the brain or whatever tortures might happen behind a door. Soldier after soldier chose the bullet, not knowing that the Commandant had decided he would grant life and freedom to any prisoner whose courage allowed him to face whatever waited unknown behind the door. On the other sides of that door was freedom, but POWs chose certain death because they feared the gamble. Fear of risking kills us!

2. **Lack of Commitment.** Have you chosen to be committed? How much more can you commit to things that really matter in life? *Will* you, or are you going to *try?*

3. **Savior.** Do you find people to save and cover up for their failures and shortcomings? Are you a chronic rescuer/enabler?

4. **Victim.** Are you blaming others for your challenges? Do you invite people to your pity party by looking for sympathy?

5. **Indecisiveness.** Up until now, have you been infected with the paralysis of analysis? Do you feel afraid or incapable to decide?

6. **Low expectations.** Do you expect too little from yourself and others—handicapping your team by lowering the bar?

7. **Fear of failure.** Do you pull back from participating because you might make a mistake or appear to be imperfect?

8. **Closed-minded.** How do your blinders fit, and how do they feel? Are you open to new learning, experiences, and opportunities?

9. **Critical.** No matter what's going right, do you look for what's wrong? Are you quick to find fault? Do you belong to the *Ginsu* family—always slicing and dicing?

10. **Lack of Focus.** Have you lost your concentration because you've lost your Focus? Are you expending your energy on what truly matters?

11. **Wanting to be liked.** Are you unable to say what you think because it might ruffle some feathers? Do you hide who you are?

12. **Low self-worth.** Have you disqualified yourself from success because you think you're not capable? Don't you deserve it?

13. **Low self-esteem.** Do you feel you deserve the bad things that happen to you? Do you accept abuse or punish yourself?

14. **Focusing on problems.** Is your Focus on what you can do or what you *can't?* Is your glass half-full or half-empty?

15. **Controlling vs. empowering.** Are you a dictator or an empowering leader who uses

constructive criticism and compliments?

16. **Having to work hard.** Do you work so you won't have to deal with what's at home, or with something else that's lacking in your life?

17. **Having to be perfect.** Must all the lights be green before you leave your driveway? Do you hesitate to act until all is known?

18. **Fear of rejection.** Are you a people-pleaser who needs validation, acceptance, and popularity in order to feel successful?

19. **Fear of embarrassment.** Are you overly concerned with what other people think? Do you wear a mask because you don't want people to see the spontaneous, "real" you?

20. **Lack of Purpose.** Do you ever feel like a sailboat with a great mast and no rudder? Are you at the mercy of the wind, unable to take control or guide your life?

Perhaps another false belief or unhealthy habit is holding you back, but it's probably based in this list if you'll think about it.

What is holding you back? On the following chart, identify and circle false beliefs that are pulling you back from your true vision. They can upset your current reality and rob you of current success. How can you be untied from them?

131

Identify the enemy

Substitute teachers understand the value of knowing students' names—when your "enemy" is identified, you gain an advantage! Know a disruptive student's name and you wield power! The same is true with other challenges you face. Accurately identify the enemy, and you'll know which weapons to use.

WHAT'S HOLDING ME BACK?

my false beliefs   my true vision

my current reality

Fear of risking	Wanting to be liked
Lack of Commitment	Low self-worth
See myself as a savior	Low self-esteem
See myself as a victim	Focusing on problems
Fear of deciding	Controlling vs empowering
Low expectations	Having to work hard
Fear of failure	Having to be perfect
Closed-minded	Fear of rejection
Critical	Fear of embarrassment
Lack of Focus	Lack of Purpose
_____	_____
other	other

CHAPTER 6: **COMMITMENT!**

NOTES TO
MYSELF

This is why you went through the last exercise. Your *true vision* pulls you toward success while your *false beliefs* pull you toward failure. They defeat you in the dark. Calling them out into open light takes away their power to sneak up and undermine your Commitment.

I love the saying, "I have met the enemy, and he's living in my shorts!" Your Commitment depends on hearing *true vision* in your self-talk. You would never tolerate people saying to you the negative things you say to yourself!

In our *Leadership Adventure* classes, participants identify obstacles that are holding them back. Then we use some great techniques to confront these *false beliefs* that are limiting their success. One participant was able, for the first time, to look at his fears and mock them for how weak they really were. Examining their threats and hearing their lies, he saw his enemies clearly and taunted them back: "Is that *all* you've got?"

How about the *false beliefs* that whisper failure in *your* ear? Don't be afraid to hear them —just remember that they are lies. Maybe, at one time in your life, they had some element of truth, but that was *then* and this is *now*. Anything they can throw at you is nothing when you put it in the context of *up until now.* Remember, you are "Under Construction!"

Facing *false beliefs* in your life can teach you how to become free, so you *can* keep your commitments. Have you ever planned to go on an exercise program or lose some weight? Certainly, you were sincere, but you were no longer committed at the time you gave up! If you had really been committed, you'd still be doing what you committed to do, right? Commitment at the point of decision is true commitment!

Have you ever *wanted* to quit smoking? Mark Twain said it was easy to quit—he'd done it *hundreds* of times! Many people keep quitting but never quit. Here's a real-life story that will help you identify the enemy if smoking is something you've been *trying* to quit:

Years ago, my cowriter, Chris Carey, was involved in staging a hypnosis show for Australia's famous Sydney Opera House. After the performances, the hypnotist offered to help anyone who wanted to lose weight or quit smoking. Chris was amazed at the success stories people told him after a session with the hypnotist. The way it worked was explained to him this way: *willpower* is not as strong as *habit,* and willpower is the area in which most people fail. However, as the hypnotist explained it, *imagination* is often stronger than habit, because it allows the subject to experience mentally what success will be like. The track is laid down to follow again and again.

So the hypnotist's secret was freeing people's minds to *imagine* what life would be like when their goal was met. People were able to commit to a clear picture of success because their imaginations provided one for them to believe in and, therefore, commit to. They knew what their "house" looked like (see Chapter 2).

I'm not saying you need a hypnotist to rid you of your unhealthy habits and false beliefs. I'm saying if you struggle with keeping your commitments, you should ask yourself if you know what your goal feels like, what it sounds like. If not, no amount of willpower will aid your ability to keep your Commitment. You need Vision to do that—and that's another chapter!

Right before your eyes

"The moment one definitely commits oneself, the Providence moves too. All sorts of things occur to help that would never otherwise have occurred," wrote W. H. Murray. "A stream of events issues from the decision, raising unforeseen incidents and meetings and material assistance, which no man could have dreamt would come his way."

In other words, everything begins to move at the sound of Commitment. It may not happen immediately where you can see it for yourself, but events and opportunities start coming together in amazing ways. First, you need to know what you want; next, create a path to get it; and then, just commit to *Live It!*

Maybe this phenomenon is like when you decide to buy a certain car and, suddenly, you see that model everywhere you go. You notice what you're looking for. You gain an extra set of eyes when you commit, and you see opportunities you may have passed over before.

At the same time, your Commitment begins calling to other people. You meet people who can be helpful resources because they're looking for what you've got or they've committed to the same thing.

But when you un-commit, the positive things that are happening start moving away. Guard your Focus when you're tempted to pull back—are you seeing your *true Vision* clearly enough that you can commit to it? You can waste time fighting an enemy you *think* is lack of Commitment when you should be fighting your *real* enemy, which could be lack of Focus or Vision. Remember: Identify your enemy so you'll know how to fight it.

Some of the people who come to our train-ing sessions never think of themselves as leaders because their false beliefs and poor performance in the past make them feel disqualified. B. C. Forbes explains it: "Many a man has walked up to the opportunity for which he has long been preparing himself, looked it full in the face, and then begun to get cold feet.... When it comes to betting on yourself and your power to do the thing you know you must do or write your-self down as a failure, you're a chicken-livered coward if you hesitate."

Some of us have felt like "chicken-livered cowards" because of our past failures and hesi-tations. Learning how to use these six tools in your tool box will help you repair your past and build your future.

I'm using a lot of quotations from success-ful people in this chapter because I want you to understand that these are not Scott Black's copy-righted ideas. They're not new. They're very old, rooted in common sense. For whatever reason, common sense isn't so common anymore.

Commitment is key—and when you lose your Commitment, you lose your confidence as well as your self-respect, your energy as well as your momentum, your followers as well as the ambitions that drew them.

137

BECOMING YOUR DREAMS

Whom do you trust?

In our classes, participants need to trust each other. We ask them to make one of three statements to each individual, adding no other comment. Knowing very little about each other, they look in each other's eyes and say out loud:

- I trust you, *or*
- I don't trust you, *or*
- I don't know.

Some people trust without thinking, while others think without trusting. We also tell them to "trust the process" (because they don't understand yet that the course is actually designed for their success). Their Commitment lessens when they come up against parts of the process they don't yet understand.

Without trust in the person who nominated them to attend, they would quit. Without trust in the incredible life changes they've seen in their friend's life, they'd miss out on one of the most powerful events in their lives. Whom or what do you trust in? When you commit to your clear Vision, your trust will pay off.

Commitment isn't a "sometime" thing—it must be consistent and reliable.

In battle, Commitment counts. General Sir John Monash said, "I don't give a damn for your logical service when you think I am right; when I really want it most is when you think I am wrong." General George S. Patton said, "Wars may be fought with weapons, but they are won by men. It is the spirit of the men who follow, and of the man who leads, that gains the victory." Armies function on Commitment to their country, their cause, and their corps. Commitment is all about trust.

In business, if your team members can't trust you, will they follow you through tough situations? Most people pull back when they hit resistance, but committed leaders push through walls—even when others call them fools or jump ship. Even when ridicule and humility become the consequences of Commitment, leaders know that when they stay committed, walls yield and people follow.

You could be doing a lot of things wrong and occasionally fall short of people's expectations. You might be recognized as the flawed human being you really are. But when you are truly committed—Heart, Body and Soul—your team will see your Commitment, and that will help fuel their own fires. Commitment can cover a multitude of leadership "sins." It doesn't sanction or excuse them, but it gives a team reasons to focus on more than weaknesses.

Commit to yourself

Sad to say, committed leadership isn't always acknowledged gratefully. A good example of what a committed leader must sometimes endure is in the following parable:

A mule fell into a farmer's well, and the farmer heard the mule braying. The farmer sympathized with the old mule but, after carefully assessing the situation, he decided neither the mule nor the well was worth the trouble of saving. Instead, he called his neighbors together and enlisted their help hauling dirt to bury the mule in the well and end his misery.

Of course, the old mule became hysterical as the neighbors shoveled and clumps of dirt hit his back. Then it dawned on him that every time a load of dirt landed on his back, he should shake it off and take a step up!

This he did, blow after blow. "Shake it off and step up...shake it off and step up...shake it off and step up," he repeated to encourage himself. No matter how painful the blows or how distressing the situation, he fought his urge to panic and kept shaking it off and stepping up.

Well, you probably know how this story ends. It wasn't long until the old mule, battered and exhausted, stepped triumphantly over the wall of that well! What threatened to bury him actually delivered him, because of the way he chose to handle his adversity.

At Empower U, we explain that when you're committed to your Vision, you'll encounter resistance. As you move toward your dreams, some of this dirt will knock you on your butt. You have to pick yourself, dust yourself off, and hit it again and again and again. After all, what do you want—sympathy? Or do you want to become your dreams?

Commitment to endure the blows and keep stepping up is a key for your survival too. The farmer gave up on saving the mule, even after years of faithful service. If the mule had given up and laid down, he would have died. He had to save himself *in* his situation—no one was going to pull him *from* it.

Notice that the mule's Commitment worked *in* his problem to find a solution. There was no one else working for his survival. Like it or not, he had to become the leader and take control of his own life. Once the farmer and his neighbors saw that a solution was in the works, they began shovelling harder, faster, and more enthusiastically, because they saw that it just might work. In your situation, when people seem to be working to bury you, your Commitment may lead them to elevate you instead!

141

Commit carefully

Finally, let me encourage you to commit cautiously. Are you *required* to commit to everyone who asks for your Commitment? No. Your Commitment belongs to your convictions. You commit because of your character and integrity, not because it is convenient or popular. Commitment is tied to who you are as a man or a woman. Once you give it, you must *Live It*.

Once you have truly committed, you can stop thinking about "if" you are and focus on "how" you can fulfill your pledge. If you must renegotiate your Commitments, always do so in a timely manner before your action is required.

In *Leadership Awakening*, we say there are three types of people in this world: those who make things happen, those who watch things happen, and those who wonder, "What the heck just happened?" Make the Commitment to which type you will be. Make things happen!

The second Secretary General of the United Nations was Dag Hammarskjold, a man of great Commitment and character. He wrote, "There is a point at which everything becomes simple and there is no longer any question of choice, because all you have staked will be lost if you look back. Life's point of no return."

Commitment: it's what leaders live.

My face is set, my gait is fast,
my goal is Heaven, my road is narrow,
my way is rough, my companions are few,
my guide is reliable, my mission is clear.
I cannot be bought, compromised, detoured,
lured away, turned back, diluted, or delayed.
I will not flinch in the face of sacrifice,
hesitate in the presence of adversity,
negotiate at the table of the enemy,
ponder at the pool of popularity,
or meander in a maze of mediocrity.
I won't give up, shut up, let up, or slow up.

Robert Moorehead

To laugh often and love much; to win the respect of intelligent persons and the affection of children; to earn the approbation of honest critics and endure the betrayal of false friends; to appreciate beauty; to find the best in others; to give of one's self; to leave the world a bit better, whether by a healthy child, a garden patch or a redeemed social condition; to have played and laughed with enthusiasm and sung with exultation; to know even one life has breathed easier because you have lived... this is to have succeeded!

— Ralph Waldo Emerson

CHAPTER 7:
TEAM!

team \tēm\ *n* 1: a group on the same side, as in a game. 2: a group organized to work together. 3: A vehicle along with the animal or animals harnessed to it. 4: A brood or flock.

Success is a team sport. You don't achieve it alone, and even if you could, you'd discover you can't celebrate it alone.

Before attending our *Leadership Awakening* and *Leadership Adventure* classes, many students have never seen what a committed team can accomplish. We start with a group of strangers from different backgrounds and all walks of life, and they form a united team to accomplish individual and group goals. We don't do this just so they can make a bunch of new friends—many of them never see each other again. The bigger reason is so they can see how important real teams are out there in the day-to-day world.

If strangers can build a winning and committed team over only three days, how much better a team can they build with members of their family? With the people who really matter in their lives? With their churches, synagogues, temples, or mosques? In their communities, schools, and organizations? In their vocations?

These aren't just "warm fuzzy" questions. Sure, it's nice to think what a better world we'd have if more people knew how to contribute and work cooperatively. But, assuming we agree on the concept, why don't we see teamwork being demonstrated more often? I want to use this chapter to convince you that its practical demonstration depends on *your* effective leadership.

In every team, a "culture" develops over time. Sometimes it evolves accidentally, but such cultures tend to be reactive rather than proactive. Other times, the team's culture is imposed by decree, according to the dictates of a single individual. In that case, one person responds and everyone else reacts. I'm suggesting that neither of these cultures is healthy.

I prefer a third model, in which a purposeful culture is defined by consensus, care, and respect, drawing from and responding to the best of each member's values and contributions to create a whole greater than the sum of its parts—or a team better than just the skills of its members.

A team needs a leader, but should it always look to the same leader in every situation? In many teams, one person leads by default—he or she took a step forward and everyone else took a step back. *Leadership Awakening* and *Leadership Adventure* show us that anyone can lead in influencing a team's culture. It's every team member's obligation to be proactive and share in leadership when it's appropriate. Here are four skills of outstanding leaders and managers:

TOP LEADERS AND MANAGERS:

- **Define the right outcomes.**
  Establish clear objectives, so employees know exactly what they need to attain, then allow them to accomplish their goal in a way that is best for them. Do not define the steps to reach the goal.

- **Select for talent.**
  Identify the talents needed for a position, then find people who fit that role. Look beyond a person's knowledge and skills, and size up how they will fit the job, their attitude, etc.

- **Focus on strength.**
  Bring out what is already there, rather than working to put in something that is missing. Most gains made on weaknesses will be short-lived. Build on strengths.

- **Find the right fit.**
  Talent never becomes talented without being given a role in which it can shine. Give people an opportunity to succeed in areas in which they are strong.

Some readers will look at this and say, "Scott's lost it—he's just given us a recipe for chaos!" I'm not saying every team member should have identical authority or responsibility. I'm saying every team member must learn to be a leader in his or her area of authority—even if they're only responsible for meeting their commitments to team members. Some workers yield even this personal responsibility and then complain that they don't feel valued in their jobs. Many people who attend our courses are amazed to find out how powerful and capable of decisive self-leadership they really are.

Look at those four leadership skills again, and see how you can apply them right now:

- *Define the right outcomes* for yourself and your teammates. Accomplish the goal by using steps that work well for you, so you won't always be workers who must be led.
- *Select for talent.* Recognize and use the talents, knowledge, skills, attitude, and fit among those already on your team. See your own talent and call it forth instead of waiting for someone else to do that for you.
- *Focus on strengths* and bring out positive traits and skills in others. Use your abilities to coach and encourage.
- *Find the right fit.* Recognize opportunities for you and others to succeed in areas of strength.

You and I are always being watched by people looking for leadership examples. Whether or not you have a leadership title, you owe it to your team to participate with Passion—Heart, Body, and Soul!

Here are two charts to help you determine whether your best response is to follow or lead in specific situations:

LEADER/FOLLOWER RESPONSE GRID

	Leader	Follower
Active	Sees an opportunity—chooses to respond by leading	Sees an opportunity—chooses to respond by following and offering support to the leader
Passive	Sees an opportunity—chooses not to respond	Sees an opportunity—chooses not to respond, contribute, or follow

LEADER/FOLLOWER ACTION CYCLE

HOW TO CHOOSE YOUR CONTRIBUTIONS:

1. **Perceive the situation objectively.**
   a. Where are we now?
   b. Where are we going?
   c. What will it take to get there? And how long?

2. **Evaluate your ability to lead and/or actively follow in terms of this situation.**

3. **Choose either to lead or actively follow.**

4. **Identify contributions and specific action steps.**

5. **Evaluate your contributions in your current situation.**

6. **Take action.**

Depending on the situation, this entire process might take only 10 seconds—or it might take a week. Each situation is unique, as is each member of the team. Take into account all data, including time allotted for decisions, team members' personality styles, safety, strengths, weaknesses, experience, history, etc.

Are there ever valid reasons why people choose not to lead? Of course there are. Here are a few:

- An individual may already be committed as a leader in other aspects. Leadership in this role might dilute effectiveness in other areas.

- An individual may believe someone else will be more effective as a leader in this situation.

- An individual isn't interested in reaching out to lead others in this particular situation or using this particular method.

- An individual has decided it's time for someone else to step forward and lead. Leadership can't be passed on if only one person has developed these skills.

There are also invalid reasons people use to avoid leadership. Here are some of those:

- An organization is set up so that only managers or designated individuals with certain titles are allowed to take on leadership responsibilities.

- An individual lacks confidence in his or her own abilities to lead.

- An individual may be encountering internal walls or barriers to effective leadership:

- shutting down
- emotionally hijacked
- noncommunicative
- vindictive
- fear ("False Evidence About Reality"
  based in an inaccurate belief system)
- An individual may not be a committed team player.

There's a saying: "Teamwork makes the dream work." One of the best ways to get someone to join *your* team is to let them know you're on *their* team. Then there is only one team.

Leadership isn't positional; it's not *where* you are. It's what you *do* where you are.

What do you see?

In *Leadership Awakening,* participants have an opportunity to tell their team members two leadership qualities they see in them. Of course, it's good for the team member to hear it; it's also great practice for the person who says it.

Many managers and would-be leaders forget how important it is to recognize good things and not just point out needed improvements. As a leader of people, it's important that you have balance, acknowledging and focusing on others' strengths while being aware of weaknesses. Look for opportunities to build people.

151

Later on, participants also tell team members a way in which they see them holding back. They speak carefully, so their words will be valued and the teammate will succeed.

In both instances, the listener's response is limited to "Thank you." Wow! What if your job's team rules were similar? What if your team members spoke up about things that are praiseworthy and coached each other with care to succeed? And what if we responded with appreciation instead of defensiveness?

We've all seen people do things and said, "I want to be just like them." At other times, we've thought, "I would never do that!" Are you an example of what to do or what not to do? Remember, what people see you do speaks so loudly, they may not be able to hear what you say.

In one of his seminars, Chris asks audience members to look at their left hand and study it intently. In 15 seconds, he challenges each person to find something on their hand they have never noticed before. It could be a cut or a scratch, a callous from their ring, even a new wrinkle! *Hands* are constantly changing, and so are *people*.

Yet, we tend to see people one way, in terms of hang-ups and hassles, problems and procedures. As similar as we all are, each of us is unique, and we're all changing day-to-day. Using "new eyes," we need to see friends, spouses, children, coworkers, clients, and even strangers, as the unique and ever-changing people they are.

NOTES TO MYSELF

Over the days our participants meet together, I've noticed how their faces seem to change. Maybe they really don't change—maybe I do. I start seeing them *personally*. They become *real* to me. Is this happening for you at your work? Every person you meet has a personal story with triumphs and tragedies. They have needs they must meet. In fact, they are more *like* you than *different* from you. Can you *see* it? Do you *say* it?

See how Chris's "hand philosophy" plays out in the charts on the next two pages, as we look at "business culture." We define this as the human side of a business: the hearts and minds of an organization's people, their habits, beliefs, attitudes and the way they interact with each other. Business culture is the values that underlie all decision-making. It is the foundation for all relationships with your customers, both internal and external. Business culture can best be defined as the way things are done in your business. Does your business recognize the strengths and value of its individual contributors?

COMPARISONS OF BUSINESS CULTURES:	
A WEAK CULTURE	**A STRONG CULTURE**
As a weak leader, I create a negative environment.	As a strong leader, I create a positive environment.
I am a dictator.	I am a motivator.
I am controlling.	I allow for creativity.
I use fear to keep people in line—fear of loss, fear of risk, fear of rejection.	My empowerment and encouragement support my team.
Backbiting and office politics are common.	Members of my team support each other.
The environment is stressful and nobody is having fun.	My team is committed and we can feel the enthusiasm.
The only time employees hear from me is when I think they've done wrong.	I give compliments on a job well done and constructive criticism in needed areas.
I lack respect for workers, who are manipulated and treated like tools.	I pinpoint personalities and treat workers like valuable assets.
I find resistance and opposition to change.	I welcome input from all for continual improvement.

Organizations have both managers and leaders, playing important roles in the success of an organization. A business' culture determines the roles that leaders, managers, and workers play in the organization. A team's effectiveness not only depends on how much energy is expended, but also on whether or not the energy put forth is in the "right jungle," as Stephen Covey says. With all the changes taking place in our families, communities, companies, and country, we need leadership first and management second.

MANAGEMENT VERSUS LEADERSHIP:

MANAGERS	LEADERS
Bottom-line focused—"How can I best accomplish certain things?"	Deal with the top line—"What are the things I want to accomplish?"
Do things right	Do the right things
Efficient at climbing the ladder of success	Determine if the ladder is leaning against the right wall
Keep the ship running, the engine oiled, and the ship in good repair	Steer the ship, decide the direction, the ship's size, characteristics and potential
Manage things	Lead people
Set up procedure manuals, work schedules, and improve technologies—they work on "how"	Articulate the vision, direction, and the underlying mission of the organization, inspiring and motivating—they work on "why"
On a farm, they make sure the crops are planted, cared for, and harvested on time	On a farm, they decide which crops to plant and whether/when any will be planted
In a jungle, they are behind the producers, sharpening machetes, working on muscle enhancement programs—figuring out the best way to compensate machete-wielders	In a jungle, they climb the tallest tree to make sure the team is heading in the right direction. They survey the entire situation and, if need be, yell, "Wrong jungle"

Portions adapted from Stephen Covey's The 7 Habits of Highly Effective People

BECOMING YOUR DREAMS

Let's personalize this information to the role you play in your organization. In Chapter 3, you wrote out your values and ways you reinforce them as an example of *how* you are already a leader. Then you wrote about your roles in life—an example of *where* you are already a leader. Next, you wrote about what you enjoy most and least in your work. And you wrote about how you can change what you don't like. You went on to describe your ideal business culture. And now, you're seeing that you do have power to implement this culture, at least within the parameters of your responsibility.

It's important to recognize that leadership is not a title but a role. You and I have certain roles in which, if we fail to lead, no one will. Managers can become so accustomed to managing that they lose opportunities to lead where they can.

Leadership assets

As a leader, your role should not be to fix people. Your role should be to give them more choices. If you become the guru, the expert, you're not supposed to be "flawed" like everybody else. Truthfully, *knowing* and *doing* are two different things, and many leaders struggle with their "inner hypocrite." A hypocrite knows to

156

do the right thing, and yet sometimes does something else. True leaders work every day to be a little bit better—and a little less hypocritical—than they have been. And they are quick to acknowledge their lack of perfection. They don't excuse their mistakes because they have a position of power, but they are willing to correct them because they have a position of responsibility.

Being a leader is not about covering your butt, as I said in Chapter 5. In our *Leadership Awakening* and *Leadership Adventure* classes, people go to great lengths to cover up their weaknesses and poor attitudes—not realizing that their teammates are already aware of them!

It's the same where you work and live. You may be the only one who still thinks you're covering well. Others know. Leadership is not about perfection. Your life as a leader is about your values, your responsibility to that big question: *What do you want?* You can't move in that direction if you're sitting on your butt or spending all your time covering it!

Leadership takes place at all levels of an organization. Every individual in a company should work to be the best he or she can be. Because leadership is action and not position, individuals in leadership positions should lead by example. When this philosophy starts at the top of an organization and filters down, it establishes a successful culture and encourages all employees to be leaders where they work. Leaders...Under Construction.

QUALITIES OF EFFECTIVE LEADERS:

Leaders have a vision and communicate it to their team.

Leaders make decisions, whether popular or not.

Leaders are role models.

Leaders make excellence their everyday concern.

Leaders live by this motto:
"Perfection is our goal. Excellence will be tolerated!"

Leaders have expectations of excellence.

Leaders stimulate an environment of creativity.

Leaders take risks; they step outside the box.

Leaders are growth- and results-oriented.

Leaders have an attitude that inspires others.

Leaders are motivators.

Leaders involve their team in their decision-making process.

Leaders focus on creative solutions.

Leaders have a mission and a vision for their areas of responsibility.

Leaders value their team members as their greatest asset.

In *Life is Tremendous,* Charles "Tremendous" Jones explains that the Law of Use and Disuse applies to character traits as well as muscles. If we don't continually exercise our leadership qualities, they get weak.

For instance, sincerity isn't something you can turn on and off. Exercise your sincerity muscles all the time—not so you can show them off, but because you need their strength. When people realize you are sincerely interested in them as a person, not just as an employee, co-worker, supplier, or customer, then doing business becomes a pleasure.

You've heard the old saying: People don't care how much you know until they know how much you care. Relationships are built genuinely—on sincerity, generosity, and integrity. Using fake or cosmetic actions to build relationships will eventually be exposed and backfire.

T.E.A.M. is a great acronym for **T**ogether, **E**verybody **A**chieves **M**ore. You've probably heard that before, just as you've also heard that there is no "**I**" in team. It sounds good, but it's a lie, or at least a false belief! If there's no "**I**" in team, there's no possibility of a "**U**" (you) in team either. And that means there's no team, unless we're talking about someone else's team!

Don't dismiss this statement as a cliché. Team success is the responsibility of each member. Sometimes the greatest demonstration of leadership is being willing to follow and participate—Heart, Body, and Soul. In other words, "**U**" must be the "**I**" in "**TEAM**"!

Leaders understand that the greatest asset of any organization or team is the hearts and minds of its people. When team members understand that they are more than just employees, more than workers who trade their hours for dollars, they'll become "missionaries" for the mission of the company. When team members are fed on an emotional level, they will serve with their hearts. They become dedicated teammates, not just employees working for a check.

The greatest mission in the world can't be accomplished without people. Most of our personal goals can't be reached without involving others. A team isn't a team without people. There's not much of a family without people. All of us are "people who need people." All the Purpose and Passion in the world will not create success without people. They are the glue and fasteners that secure the rungs on the ladder of success.

Since the majority of their waking hours are spent on the job, true leaders want "their people" to enjoy what they are doing, to buy in to their work's deeper purpose. Earlier, I quoted Clarence Francis, who wrote: "You can buy people's time; you can buy their physical presence at a given place; you can even buy a measured number of muscular motions per hour. But you cannot buy enthusiasm...you cannot buy loyalty...you cannot buy the devotion of their hearts. This you must earn."

I'm repeating this because, in building a successful business, you must learn how to access the most powerful aspects of all your assets, including the hearts and minds of people. How do you build relationships that allow you to maximize the human assets you lead?

First of all, leaders must recognize and appreciate that all people have three basic needs:

- Someone to love
- Something to learn
- Some purpose to live for

What if you could help your team find all three of these at their place of work? Even two out of three ain't bad! People want to know that they contribute to life, that who they are and what they do matters.

Next time you drive in an area where buildings and bridges are covered in graffiti, ask yourself who put it there, and why? Sadly, I think it's because these are the only places some people feel they can leave their mark.

The Gallup Organization polled more than 100,000 employees in a dozen industries, identifying 12 worker beliefs that are significant in triggering a profitable, productive workplace. Here's what employees said is most important:

12 KEY WORKER BELIEFS:

- My supervisor, or someone at work, seems to care about me as a person.

- There is someone at work who encourages my development.

- The mission/purpose of my company makes me feel my job is important.

- My coworkers are committed to doing quality work.

- I have a best friend at work.

- This last year, I have had opportunities at work to learn and to grow.

- I know what is expected of me at work.

- I have the materials and equipment I need to do my work right.

- At work, I have the opportunity to do what I do best every day.

- In the last 7 days, I have received recognition or praise for doing good work.

- It the last 6 months, someone at work has talked to me about my progress.

- At work, my opinions seem to count.

Analysis reveals a consistent and reliable relationship between these 12 worker beliefs and the bottom line in *profits, productivity, employee retention,* and *customer loyalty.* In ranking the businesses that supported these 12 beliefs, the top 25% averaged *14% higher revenues* and *10% lower turnovers* than the rest of the companies. Creating a positive culture isn't about "warm fuzzies." It's a sound business practice.

Knowing our clients

Other people play two basic roles in relation to our businesses. First, we have our internal clients. They are the team members we work with every day. These people allow us to do our jobs in a certain fashion. They contribute to who we are, what we do, and the quality in which we do it. The power of a group of people working together is phenomenal.

Second, there are our external clients. These people buy our service and/or products; they are the end users. They create opportunities for us to do what we do. Without customers and clients, we couldn't stay in business. Unless we serve them well, nothing is purchased and we have no purpose for being in business.

The relationships we have with our clients, both internal and external, determine our level of success. When our clients get value from what we do, we have a good chance of getting their business. We have an opportunity to build a relationship that allows for repeat business and even friendship.

At Empower U, our graduates are responsible for our continuing existence. 99.9% of our students are referred by graduates. At the back of this book, you can read testimonials from these "raving fans." If people don't have a meaningful, empowering experience, they don't nominate others to trust them and take the class.

Once we realize that people are the most important assets in our personal and professional lives, we can build better relationships. Our internal and external clients deserve the best of who we are.

My own company, Empower U, isn't about Scott Black, and any time I start forgetting that, I see fallout in our business. A company is about people; it's a team of committed individuals. In the words of anthropologist Margaret Mead, "Never doubt that a small group of committed individuals can change the world; indeed, it is the only thing that ever has."

The credit for our company's success belongs to the team that achieves for and serves others. Many different people have played many different roles. Some have been graduates, others friends, some staff and employees, and others have believed in our cause and assisted in various ways. Some of these people have left, some are still with us, and some have left and come back. Many different people, many different contributions. This is how a team works. By helping us out and believing in our vision, they gave others permission to do the same.

We end all of our *Leadership Awakening*

courses with Marianne Williamson's essay on personal liberation, quoted in Chapter 2. While it celebrates the Power of One, you can see that our team really succeeds when all of us celebrate its truth for every member of our team. I challenge you to become a leader in your team by recognizing and supporting the greatness in others...and in yourself.

Inoculate your team

Effective leadership and people management also requires skill in handling the negative. I've heard from crab fishermen that they toss the first crab they catch into their bucket and clamp a lid on tight. The crab will do all it can to get out of the bucket. But if two or more crabs are in the bucket, one will do everything it can to keep the other from getting out!

When you lead a team, it's up to you to set a tone and pace of positive expectation. You've got to be the real deal. That way, when a bad attitude comes along, your team can spot it for what it is. You'll do this best by modeling positive attitudes for others: Keep an open mind, and open heart, and an open door.

Here's an example of the real deal from the banking industry. Allowing counterfeit money to flow through a bank to its customers isn't good for business, so it's important for tellers to be able to spot bogus currency. Banks could circulate copies of fake bills to every branch office. And every time a new fake was discovered, they could send a copy to every teller for comparison. Then, whenever tellers took in a bill, they could thumb through their stack of fakes to see if there was a match in the money they received.

But banks don't do that! There are too many ways to fake it for any teller to recognize them all. Instead, tellers are trained so thoroughly in what a *legitimate* bill looks like that they recognize a phony when they see it. A shout goes off in their brains: "Wait a minute—*something's* not right!"

Your leadership can also establish a culture that is so positive and genuine that, when a counter attitude shows up, your teammates immediately recognize that something's not right. Caution flags go up, and people start to examine what's happening.

Here's a medical metaphor. Every day, your body fights off diseases without your even being aware. When an infection begins to invade, antibodies respond to defend their territory. In a healthy body, they repel what doesn't belong. At other times, a disease finds no foothold because its would-be host has already been inoculated against infection. What could be deadly has no impact because immunity was established ahead of time.

Negative attitudes in an organization will do the same thing. When Billy Martin took over as manager of the New York Yankees baseball team, former manager Casey Stengel gave him a valuable piece of advice: "Lump your losers together." By this, he meant that bad attitudes are contagious—quarantine them and don't let others get infected.

You get the idea, don't you? Part of leadership is helping your healthy team ward off disease. The best way to do this is by establishing a healthy diet of integrity, accountability, praise, honesty, direction, support, and feedback. Author Ken Blanchard says that feedback is the breakfast of champions!

I enjoy metaphors, as you can tell. So, while we're on a medical theme, let's look at antibodies in another way. Sometimes they must be suppressed, as in the case of a transplanted organ. When a key body organ fails to perform and its "dis-ease" threatens the rest of the body, it's necessary to remove that organ and replace it with a healthy one that can perform in its place. However, the rest of the body may view the new organ as an invader and try to elimi-

nate it. Doctors protect the transplant by providing suppressive therapy.

As a leader, it's up to you to do the same
for new team members. In *Leadership Awakening*, we have an exercise in which classmates
introduce each other to the rest of the class as
if a new employee has joined their ranks at work.
It's their task to pre-interview this new team
member and find out about their life, family,
education, experience, skills, interests and
more—and then "sell" this person to the team.

When they've finished, the rest of the class
votes on whether to accept or reject this person
as a teammate. However, their vote has *nothing*
to do with the quality of the individual; it has
everything to do with the quality of endorsement given by the person who does the
introducing. Often, good people are "eliminated"
because the person who has the responsibility
of bringing them into the team can't get the job
done. As a leader, you need to be everybody's
champion.

According to Coach Lou Holtz, there are
three questions every teammate asks of a leader:

• Can I trust you?
• Are you committed?
• Do you care about me?

NOTES TO
MYSELF

"Can I trust you?" means, are you a person of integrity and character? "Are you committed?" means, do you care about excellence and achieving our goals? "Do you care about me?" asks if am I just a way for you to get your goal, or am I safe with you?

Do you go to bat for your team? When your coworkers can answer yes to this question about you, my friend, you're on your way to a winning team.

Team: it's what leaders build!

Some men see things as they are and say why.
I dream things that never were and say why not.

— George Bernard Shaw
quoted by Robert F. Kennedy

CHAPTER 8:

VISION!

vi-sion \vĭ′-zhən\ *n* 1: (a) the faculty of sight; eyesight. (b) something that is or has been seen. 2: unusual competence in discernment or perception; intelligent foresight. 3: the manner in which one sees or conceives of something. 4: a mental image produced by the imagination. 5: the mystical experience of seeing as if with the eyes the supernatural or a supernatural person. 6: a person or thing of extraordinary beauty.

Would you leave on a weeklong trip without knowing where you were going? Would you board a plane with no idea where it was heading? Would you get in a motor boat that had no rudder?

Most people would respond with a resounding No! to these questions, yet many people are running their business or living their lives in a similar fashion. Career studies tell us that more planning goes into most people's *vacations* than their *vocations*.

When you get on a plane, you already know where you're heading. This is a ready example of what Stephen Covey has called "beginning with the end in mind." This chapter, near the end of the book, is about beginnings. To get to your desired end, you must begin correctly by knowing where you want to go and having a way of steering and course-correction.

We said in Chapter 2 that everything has two beginnings: first it comes into being mentally, and then it comes into being as a physical property. Some people say "When I see it, I'll believe it," but visionary leaders understand that *when* you believe it, *then* you'll see it.

Vision is about having a dream. It's knowing where you're going, seeing a goal—even if others see it as undoable for you, impractical for the times, or impossible to achieve—and then bringing your dream to reality.

In Chapter 6, I mentioned how, once you decide to buy a certain car, you start noticing that model everywhere you go. It's because your antenna is up and you're receiving signals that go unnoticed by others.

How do you explain this enhanced ability that suddenly allows you to tune into obscure details that others ignore? Knowing the answer will help you create and sustain the Vision you need to be a powerful leader.

All the tools you've ever needed to be a powerful leader are inside you, and the most powerful tool you have is sitting on your shoulders—your brain. Scientists tell us we use only

NOTES TO
MYSELF

3%–5% of our brain's potential. So, conversely, we're not using 95%–97% of our brain.

In class, we say, "If you had a piece of machinery that was only being used to 5% of its potential, what would you do? Get rid of it, get rid of its operator, or learn how to operate it better? The first two choices are not options when talking about your brain!"

It won't happen accidentally, but you can learn how to turn on your unused brain power. Remember the story about the guy who visited Manhattan for the first time and asked a taxicab driver, "How can I get to Carnegie Hall?" The cabbie replied, "Practice, practice, practice!" Likewise, your undeveloped ability to tap into the power of your creative, visionary mind will grow as you practice, practice, practice using your mind. Here's how:

Picture your success

At the back of your brain is a 4-inch stem containing your reticular activating system, called the "RAS" for short. It paints positive pictures—it does not understand negatives.

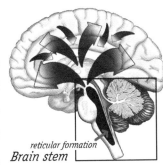

reticular formation
Brain stem

BECOMING YOUR DREAMS

To illustrate my point, close your eyes for 10 seconds—and during this time, do *not* see a picture of the Statue of Liberty in your mind. Whatever you do, *don't* picture the Statue of Liberty. Remember, no Statue. Ready? Go!

What happened when you closed your eyes? Did you see the Statue of Liberty? It's probably true that the harder you worked *not* to see it, the more vivid it became. Why? Because your RAS was at work, and it paints pictures of what your mind thinks. It doesn't hear the words *don't* or *not*. Even when you worry about what *won't* happen, your mind sees pictures of it happening, because your RAS doesn't understand *not*. That's why it's important to govern what you think about.

Also, in order for your mind not to see the Statue of Liberty, it first had to know what the monument looks like!

What if I were in your living room, backing up a large pickup truck—*work with me here!* Of course, I wouldn't want to hit your valuable antique lamp. So what would I have to keep in my field of vision so I do *not* hit it? Right— the lamp! I must *see* it to *not* hit it!

If you've played that little mind game before, you know the only way to avoid seeing the

State of Liberty is to *replace* that image with something just as vivid—maybe a bicycle-riding pink elephant wearing purple tights and juggling a baseball, a tuba, and a pizza! It's gotta be vivid!

You learn to use vivid imagery in memory improvement courses, creating highly visual images and attaching meaning to them. Then, by replaying the visual, you can remember names, places, and events.

Almost 20 years ago, Chris Carey attended a memory seminar presented by basketball legend Jerry Lucas. He mentioned the name of a woman, Eilleen Fornurakis, and Chris remembers it to this day.

Jerry painted such a visual image that it's burned into Chris' memory. Picture this lady who, according to Jerry, had a very prominent nose. He imagined that her nose was a tennis net stretching from her forehead to her chin, and on the court (the rest of her face) there was a doubles match going on—played by people holding four new racquets. Oh yes, the woman, in Jerry's image, tilted off to one side because one leg was shorter than the other.

So, what did this image create that he tied to a name? I *lean* + *four new racquets* = Eilleen Fornurakis! Using this technique, Jerry, Harry

Lorraine, and other memory experts have been able to recall the names of several hundred people when they've been introduced just once.

You've heard "in one *ear* and out the other," but probably not "in one *eye* and out the other," because the mind recalls *images* much better than words. Your RAS takes words and turns them into pictures to increase your memory— and your performance too. To your mind, a picture really is worth a thousand words!

Dr. Charles Garfield's research confirmed that most peak performers are visualizers. They *see* it before others *believe* it. For example, how many homeruns did Barry Bond hit in the 2001 season? No, not 73 homeruns, but 73,000! He knocked them out of the ball park first in his mind before he earned the homerun record out in the world. He knew what a homerun swing felt like, looked like, and sounded like.

An American prisoner of war, held in North Vietnam, played a round of golf mentally every day to keep his sanity. After five years of captivity, he returned to the U.S. and broke 80 in his first round of real play.

Your Reticular Activating System is your motivation and achievement secret. Turning your thoughts and dreams into vivid pictures will increase your Vision. The more real you make these dreams, the more real your drive will be to achieve them. Visualize what you *want* instead of what you *don't* want. Our eyes are on the front of our faces because we move in the direction of our Vision. It's how we are designed.

We do exercises in our training sessions that use active visualization in full detail. When you're thinking about your coming success, this skill will make your goals real long before you see them come to pass. This is why I've asked how your success will look, feel, smell, and sound when you've attained it. A well-developed RAS can fill in all those blanks for you.

The first time I heard of this, I thought it was a New Age or metaphysical mind trick. It's not. You do it all the time and don't even think about it. For example, when you get so angry that you shut down emotionally, it's because you paint a vivid picture in your mind and keep replaying it—what someone did to mistreat you, how they wanted to hurt or embarrass you, how the incident made you appear. And you play this movie over and over, building the emotion.

Have you ever arrived home from work without remembering exactly what you did to get there? You stopped at all the stops, turned at all the turns, and didn't even think about it. Yet you got home safely. That was accidental

177

visualization. You had driven home before and the track was in place, so you let the train take you along your old, familar pattern.

Do the same thing to create a track for success! Make your mental image of success so *real*—how you're going to attain it and what it will be like—that, when challenges come, you'll just walk through them like familiar territory because you've already been there in your mind. When you visualize, it's very important to get all the details and use all your senses.

I have a dream

Martin Luther King's famous speech, "I Have a Dream," was so full of imagery that it's one of the world's most memorable. He spoke of having been to the mountain top, like Moses, who was unable to claim the Promised Land for himself but knowing it was in reach for his people. Dr. King dreamed that one day his children would be judged not by the color of their skin but by the content of their character. Do you remember? He saw it and described it so vividly that others could see his vision. And to this day, *I* can still see it.

What is your dream? Your vision? How are you seeing it? Is it a place you're familiar with? How are you sharing it to enlist followers and colaborers? Are you selling sugar water the rest of your life, or are you changing the world?

You'll recall that your RAS doesn't speak in negative words. So, when you tell a child, "Don't spill the milk!", you may be setting them up to spill their milk—you helped them create a picture of spilt milk in their heads.

When my kids were younger, sometimes Faith would want to get her little brother, Christian, in trouble. Once they were playing when she yelled, loud enough for Dad to hear, "Christian, don't bite me!" Christian, who hadn't bitten her, suddenly decided it was a great idea! Faith planted the thought by telling him *not to do* something he wasn't doing.

So why is it that we frame so many of our *wants* as *don't wants?* I think a reason why there's no Passion in our lives is because we don't identify what we *want*. We say what we *don't want* instead. We can make lists and pages of that!

- I don't want to be in a dead end job.
- I don't want to be in a relationship going nowhere.
- I don't want to be yelled at!

Consider that when we tell people what we *don't want,* we forget to tell them what we *want*. How can they hit a target they can't see? If someone tells them not to be late, there are plenty of options. Are they allowed to be two hours early, or not supposed to show up at all if they're running late? What exactly is the *want?*

I've asked you before, what *do* you want so badly that you're willing to knock down walls and push through barriers? We *can* tell ourselves and others what we *do* want! Instead of "Don't spill the milk," how about saying "It's *okay* to keep the milk *in* the cup"? Instead of "Don't be late," how about saying "It's *okay* to be *early*"?

Okay—I just lost some readers!

In our seminars, everything happens on a schedule, but do we tell people *not* to move so slowly? No, we tell them "It's okay to *hurry!"* and we get a much better response even before we let them in on why we say it. Once they understand, it becomes an inside thing—a quick motivator.

Exercise #1 was tied into helping you identify what you want. As we noted in the first chapter, it's easier to write a list of what we *don't want* than identify what we really *do want,* but leaders with Vision speak in the positive.

What's your dream? How's your Vision? What stirs you? When you find out, you won't be hitting the snooze button a dozen times. You'll be jumping out of bed before the alarm goes off, shouting "It's a great day to be alive!"

Do you think that's extreme? Why? Betcha it's because you can't *see* yourself doing that...yet!

EXERCISE #5

Here's an exercise to do when you go to bed tonight. There's no corresponding workbook writing to go with it, so make a note now to remind you to do this:

Before you go to sleep, lie down, close your eyes, and see yourself waking up in the morning happy and refreshed. In your mind's eye, see the clock showing the time you will awaken. See and hear the alarm going off. See yourself jumping out of bed, ready to live like it's a great day to be alive!

Lay down this track to follow in the morning. Create it with your Vision, and watch it happen in your life.

Using your brain

In our *Power Goal Setting* class, I tell a story about how tribespeople in the Far East catch monkeys. According to tourist tales, when someone wants to celebrate you, they have a special dinner in your honor where they serve—and you are expected to eat—monkey brains!

181

The most interesting part of the story is the way the locals catch the monkeys. They clean out coconuts, leaving just shells with large holes in them. Then they fill the shells about a quarter full with rice and leave the coconuts lying around on the jungle floor. The monkeys come down from the trees, pick up the coconuts, put their hand inside, and grab a hand full of rice.

With their fists clenched around the rice, the holes are suddenly too small for them to pull their hands out of the coconuts. They frantically shake their hands, jump up and down, screech and strain to free themselves from the coconuts, to no avail. Then the monkeys run to a tree and attempt to escape—but they can't climb because there are coconuts stuck on their hands! When they start banging the coconuts against the tree trunk to break free, the hunters hear them and come collect their "catch."

You are probably thinking, "What a stupid animal! If the monkeys would just let go of the rice, they could escape. I'd never hold on to something that would cost me my life."

As a child, Chris heard a similar story about a little boy who got his hand stuck in the opening of an antique vase worth thousands of dollars. Rescuers poured oil into the mouth of the vase, trying to slide his hand out. Finally, just as they were resigned to breaking the vase to rescue the panicked boy, his mother said, "Now, Billy, let's try one more time—open your fingers straight out, tuck in your thumb, and relax while Mommy pulls on the vase." And Billy shouted, "Mommy, I can't do that! If I opened my fingers, I would drop my penny!"

What "pennies" are holding you back, keeping you from being as happy or successful as your desires and capabilities will allow?

We all hold on to things that could be slowly killing us or our dreams. What have you been holding on to that is keeping you from being the "George Bernard Shaw" you could be? (See Chapter 3.) What habits and doubts, what false images, what BS? In short, who or what has been making a monkey out of you?

While our *Power Goal Setting* seminar students are focusing on obstacles that have been holding them back—divorce, loss of a job, a bad economy, sickness, financial struggles—we light a bonfire, and these students release their obstacles into the fire and watch them go up in smoke. It's a powerful image for their RAS to translate into Vision.

Over my years of working with thousands of people toward their personal growth, I've come to believe that no matter how successful some-one is, they are using only a portion of their abilities. What will your life be like when you let go so you can reach 70 or 80 or even 90% of your God-given potential? When is *good nuff*, not?

Made in Japan

Do you remember when "Made in Japan" meant a product's cost *and value* were cheap? No bragging rights came with that phrase on a label!

That stigma fell away as W. Edwards Deming taught the Japanese a philosophy of business and personal growth called CANI: Constant And Never-Ending Improvement. Deming was the visionary American who came to post-World War II Japan to teach statistical quality control and management principles. You see, Deming knew a higher Vision could turn Japan around, restoring their pride as they made valuable contributions to the world's economies.

As you and I continually strive to improve who we are and what we do, as Deming's CANI approach teaches, we change our lives, and those around us, for the better. This is where our concept of "Under Construction" comes from. Better today than yesterday; more tomorrow than today.

As we've discussed, one life-altering insight that accompanies CANI and endangers our Vision is that we hold on to things in our past that don't serve us well. These are obstacles that keep us from reaching our potential—our past impedes our future!

Where does your Vision point? Is it foresight or is it hindsight? Would you drive down a freeway at 70 miles per hour while looking back over your shoulder? No, but many people live their lives this way, focusing on what's behind them—and allowing that to influence what's ahead of them. Are you holding on to fears, pain, and past experiences that limit your potential for a brighter future?

Life is a series of balancing acts. One of the most important concepts for success is this:

> Learn from the past, but don't live there. Focus on a future; create real dreams. Live in the now. So many people are living in yesterday or some distant tomorrow while today passes them by.

Take 15 minutes and honestly ask yourself this question: *What are the limiting Belief Systems that are holding me back?* Write down your answers on a separate °sheet of paper—be as honest as you know to be. Are you willing to

let those things go—or do you want to continue with your hand in a coconut and your
brains at risk? It really is your choice. You can
relax your grip on the stuff that's not helping
you any time you decide! What do you want?

Oddly, it's sometimes our past *successes,* and
not our failures, that most effectively hold us
back. For instance, I have a friend who refers to
the publication that lists our country's most
successful people as "Who's *Through* in America."
He says problems developed in his life when he
started believing his past successes (the ones
that got him included in the book) made him a
permanent success. Remember: Improvement
isn't enough—it only counts when it's Constant
And Never-Ending Improvement!

Whether it's your successes or your failures, let them go! Then, with no resistance from
your past, you can create the future that honors who you are and what you do. When you
commit to getting rid of your junk, have your
own bonfire that will also kindle your enthusiasm —and people will come from miles to watch
you burn!

Vision questions

When you are leading with Vision, you'll
see three things more clearly:

186

- Where are we now?
- Where are we going?
- What will it take to get there and how long?

Leaders have a Vision, they are dreamers. Leaders discover the unknown chasms and hidden bridges between where things are and where things would better be. Without a Vision, that would be impossible; there would be nothing to move toward.

The *Bible* tells us, "Where there is no vision, the people perish...." *(Proverbs 29:18)*. An Old Testament prophet was commanded to "write the vision and make it plain on tablets, so he may run who reads it" *(Habakkuk 2:2)*.

So, if we accept the *Bible's* wisdom, we know Vision is important for life, and a leader needs to articulate it—make it clear. It's not enough just to say, "I know the way. Follow me!" It's seeing and then communicating clearly that provides direction.

Vision: it's what leaders see.

Man does not simply exist, but always decides what his
existence will be, what he will become
in the next moment.

— Viktor Frankl

CHAPTER 9:
PURPOSE!

purpose \pûr′pəs *n*\ 1: the idea or ideal kept before the mind as an end of effort or action; plan; design; aim. 2: the particular thing to be affected or attained; practical advantage or result; consequence. 3: settled resolution; determination, constancy. 4: purport; intent, as of spoken or written language. 5: a proposition; proposal; question at issue. — **on purpose** with previous design; intentionally.

This chapter is about living *with* Purpose and living *on* Purpose. Once, in describing the potential of a young person to a would-be employer, Chris remarked, "He's a pile of possibilities." I guess that meant he had a lot to work with but it hadn't been sorted out yet. The young prospect hadn't discovered his Purpose.

Most of us have heard that the journey of a thousand miles begins with a single step. The truth is that it begins with a single step and a map! Purpose explains *why* you're on your journey, so you can understand which way to go. It provides direction—while Vision lights the way, Team builds strength, Commitment steadies the course, Focus steers clear of detours, and Passion creates the energy.

189

So let's look at your Purpose. Why do you work where you do? How did you pick your career? Did "mill-town mentality" dictate your choice? (A mill town's distinguishing feature is that people have become dependent on just a few options for their livelihoods. As a result, it's assumed that future generations will join the "family business," which is working at the mill as previous generations have. It's as far as anyone's borders or aspirations reach.)

Mill-town thinking doesn't take into account anyone's special gifts, talents, interests, attitudes, and values. The big city version may be seen in the area we decide to live in, the college we attend, the type of person we date and marry, the career we choose—even the car we drive ("Dad always drove Chryslers!").

Like crabs in a box, even well-meaning parents and friends can discourage you from finding your Purpose with comments that pull you back down inside the box. It's vitally important that leaders get on with their Purpose—the world needs what you've got!

In a recent survey, half the people working in *technical* fields responded that, if they could start over again, they would get a degree in one of the *arts*. Their choices were making them a living but not a life. They didn't know what would make them happy and fulfilled when they started down their career path, and they feel stuck.

Fire up your RAS and picture half the people you know working at their jobs with only half interest, half-energy, and half-heart! Picture them as cardboard cutouts at work, with the bottom of the image missing—representing the half that didn't make it to work! As in Chapter 4, these people are only busting rocks while those who know their Purpose are building cathedrals.

My next question goes back to Chapter 3: If you're just going around in a figure-8 pattern, is it by choice or by chance? Are you in the driver's seat of your life, or are you a passenger? When are you going to discover your Purpose and direction?

The dash of your life

We noted earlier that life is what happens to us while we are making other plans. Don't let your life happen without you!

I've written a poem called "The Dash of Your Life," based on a story that has circulated for years. It refers to the small dash on your tombstone, placed between your birth date and the day you die. There's not much to the dash, but it represents all the time you lived in between.

BECOMING YOUR DREAMS

THE DASH OF YOUR LIFE

I know of a man who chose to speak
at a gathering of family and friends...
He spoke of a friend no longer there...
who, not long ago, had been.
In a box at the front of the room
his friend lay, his final bed.
Tears flowing...speaking words of wisdom...
this is what he said:

"There is the date of our birth
and the day that we die—
In the 'space between'
our 'Dash of Life' does lie.
The way that we live on this Earth—
this becomes our Dash...
When you live life like it matters,
it matters not the cars, the house, the cash.
Think about that...
are there things you'd like to change?
The 'Time is Now'—you could be
at the end, or mid-dash range.
You can't control the length of your Dash—
this is for God to divine...
The width...intensity...this is yours—
no butt prints in the Sands of Time.
What will you do today?
Every day's like a ticking clock.
How will you spend your time...
before your time in the box?
When your Eulogy is written...
life's actions rehashed,
It's okay to be proud of the things they say—
'bout how you spent your Dash."

Scott V. Black

I was thinking about this poem when I realized that none of us can control the length of our dash; it could be a sprint or a marathon. What we can control is its *width* and its *depth*. How wide and deep do you want to grow?

At Empower U, we produce our own music for the seminars. We recorded a song called "The Dash of Life," and its chorus repeats the phrase, "Planes crash and people die in the blink of an eye...," speaking to the point that we don't know how long we'll live, so live life like it matters.

My daughter Faith, then 5, loved the song. Shortly after the 9-11 events, she went to school humming it. Her teacher called me, very concerned, to tell me my little girl seemed to be obsessed with death. I told her, "Oh no, she's singing that song because she's obsessed with *life!*"

John Denver recorded a song called "I Want to Live." Do you remember its chorus?

> *I want to live*
> *I want to grow*
> *I want to see*
> *I want to know*
> *I want to give*
> *All I can give*
> *I want to be*
> *I want to live.*

BECOMING YOUR DREAMS

Chris has a friend in his mid-70s who has been diagnosed with terminal cancer. When he saw him last year, Chris asked about his health. The man pulled him into a tight hug and winked. "Chris," he confided, "we're all terminal."

It's the truth—nobody gets out of here alive! That shouldn't be a surprise to you. A time is coming when you and I will be lying on our deathbed, and we're going to ask ourselves, "Did it matter?"

Has it mattered so far that you've been on this planet, at this time, in your body, taking up space? When you're lying there, it will be too late for *shoulding* all over yourself—and yes, it's as messy as it sounds!

"I *shoulda* married that person I loved."
"I *shoulda* started that business."
"I *shoulda* spent more time with my kids."
"I *shoulda* been patient with my spouse."
"I *shoulda*, I *shoulda*, I *shoulda*...!"

You've been to funerals or seen them on television. When there's a viewing, you can walk right up to the casket and look at the departed. And they usually look *really good!*

When I see that, I ask myself one question: "Why?" When it's my time to die, I want to look like I've lived, with wrinkles everywhere! I hope my hair's falling out and my teeth are worn out because I've lived my life with *every ounce* of my life force and passion.

Many people are afraid to get too high or too low, so they live in a flat line. (Ask your doctor what a flat line means!) So many people are "saving it." For what? So they can look pretty in a box?

Life is worth more than just taking up space. You have a mission to accomplish, and it's all tied up in your life's Purpose, your *why*. Your Purpose is your whole reason for being! What is it? Why are you here? I don't mean where you are right now as you read this book. I mean, why are you on this planet? What's your Purpose?

Please understand that, like my daughter, Faith, I'm not obsessed with dying—I'm obsessed with *living*, and I want you to live too! Remember, when you live your life like it matters, it does!

When people die, their epitaph is sometimes published in the newspaper. It's an attempt to convey their accomplishments in a few paragraphs. At their funeral, different information is presented. A eulogy emphasizes what their life *meant* beyond what they *did*. It captures "snapshots" of the best parts of their lives.

BECOMING YOUR DREAMS

What do you want said in your eulogy? I'm not asking about your *achievements* but your *contributions:*

- What kind of spouse have you been?
- What kind of parent?
- What kind of son or daughter?
- What kind of friend and neighbor?
- What kind of coworker, leader, or partner?
- Who were you an example and model for?
- How did you use your time?
- Where did you serve?
- Which things were important to you?
- When were you helpful?
- Why did you matter to those around you?

Will your loved ones have to make up lies when they speak about you, or will their true remembrances reveal that you lived life to the fullest and brought life to everyone who knew you? Again, you can't decide the *length* of your dash, but you control its *depth* and its *width*.

Discover your purpose

Nietzsche said, "He who has a *why* to live can bear almost any *how*." That understanding sustained Dr. Victor Frankl, who spent years in the Auschwitz concentration camp during World War II. He saw many people slaughtered and killed, including his immediate family. After the

196

war, he wrote *Man's Search for Meaning,* in which he said hope is crucial to human survival.

Purpose provides hope and meaning. What's your Purpose? What are you living for? Why are you on this planet? Why are you living *now?* Are you taking up space, or do you know your Purpose and reason for being here? Is there something you were you put here to do?

Or do you think your Purpose is just to go to work, make money, eat, and sleep for 80 years and then you're dust?

This chapter is especially important to me because I believe there's a reason you were given this gift called life. And no matter how good or bad your life is, someone else has one that's better, and another has one that's worse.

Let's find out about your Purpose. You should know why you're here!

EXERCISE #6

This exercise is designed to help you get in touch with who you are. It's almost identical to Exercise #1, except this question is "Who am I?"

Who do you think you are? This is one of the most important questions you'll ever answer. "I'm a committed partner or friend." "I'm a loyal team member." "I'm a passionate spouse." You *must* know who you are, so you *need* to complete this exercise! Even if you don't feel inspired after thinking about your death, you've come too far to cheat yourself now.

Here's what we'll do: Go back to your private spot where you can be alone with your notebook and pen. This process won't happen for you unless you get away by yourself. Once you are in your private spot, note the time. Open your notebook to a blank sheet of paper, and at the top, write: *"I am...."*

Then, for three minutes, as you did before, rush-write what comes to your heart and mind in answer to the question "Who am I?" This means you will write and write and write. Don't stop. Don't edit—don't even think about whether your words are making sense. Just let it flow. Do not take your pen off the paper unless you have to. Keep writing—nonstop! "I am...a *father*. I am...a *husband*. I am...a...." Just write whatever comes to you that answers the question.

Before you go any further in this book, stop reading and do Exercise #6. Start now.

Did you do it? This *is* a different process from Exercise #1. Then, we said it's not as important *what* you wrote as that you wrote *something*. In this case, *what* you write is very important. You're looking your life and destiny in the eye, and it's not the time for *good nuff*. If you haven't written down answers to "Who am I?," this is your final opportunity. Go for it!

When your three minutes of rush-writing are up, stop and breathe deeply. Let go of tension. Take a moment—this was your warm-up. Once more, *trust this process!* Check your time again. This time, when you write, fill up at least three more pages as you spend the next five minutes rush-writing *"I am...."*

You're alone with your thoughts, your life-to-date, and your future. There's no one looking over your shoulder or evaluating what you write. *Who are you?* You're not just writing your eulogy —you're writing your life. Tell it now!

Before you go any further in this book, stop reading and complete the exercise. Do it now.

Inventory time

At funerals and memorial services, eulogies portray people at their best. They tell about the "Dash" and show how that person's life mattered. Chances are the words you rush-wrote convey how you want your life to end best. How wide and how deep did you see your dash?

BECOMING YOUR DREAMS

You have just created a map to reach your goal of becoming the individual you described because now you can begin with the end in mind. Now, answer these questions about your Purpose:

AM I A ROLE MODEL?

Why am I, or why am I not, a role model?

WOULD I WORK WITH A LEADER LIKE ME?

Why would I want or not want to work with me?

EXERCISE #7

High school students often are assigned to write their epitaphs, the little sayings that go on tombstones after the "Dash." I've always found that depressing, while I find a eulogy inspiring.

How do you want to be remembered? Your answers on the opposite page really described *who* you are more than *what* you do. A role model is not an action or an event; a role model is a person. A leader others want to work with is not a force or a motivation; a leader is a person.

Your eulogy will tell people who you were rather than what you did. So **Exercise #7** is about your eulogy. How do you want to be remembered? What would you like your spouse to tell about you? What tributes do you hope your children, your friends, your coworkers, and your customers will stand and say? How will they tell others your life mattered? You will have 10 minutes to summarize what you've written so far:

What do you *want?*

Who are you?

What *qualities* mean the most in your life?

What are your greatest *strengths* and *talents?*

What are your most important *relationships?*

How do you make a *difference?*

What do you *believe?*

BECOMING YOUR DREAMS

What did I *achieve?*

What have I *overcome?*

What did I *envision, imagine?*

How did I fill in my *Dash?*

This is no time to hold back—it's your life we're talking about now! Create a eulogy that describes everything you want your life to be. You will fail this assignment if you treat it lightly or don't find yourself deeply touched by the reality of your own life and death. If the thought of what you're living for doesn't bring on chills and thrills, I question if you're alive even now.

Before you go any further, get out your writing paper again and begin Exercise #7. Take only 10 minutes to pull your life together. What is your life about? What is it for? How do you make a difference?

When you are finished, read your eulogy aloud to yourself. Does it cover your dreams and goals? Does it reveal the qualities of character you displayed in achieving them? Read it again. This assignment isn't about anyone else but you. It's about your ability to live a life that matters, that makes its mark in your world, in your time. It's about *Becoming Your Dreams.* If you like what you've written, then *Want It, Create It, Live It!*

CHAPTER 9: **PURPOSE!**

Your mission statement

NOTES TO
MYSELF

Your eulogy represents the best possible you, and so will your mission statement, creating the ideal outcome and seeing yourself in the future.

Your next assignment is to turn your eulogy into a mission statement. What you wrote about the way you want to be remembered identified your Purpose: why you believe you're here and what you need to accomplish before you leave.

Your mission statement describes how you will live out your Purpose. If you've never written one before, this is a good time to begin. If you've done it in the past, this is the perfect time to reexamine your conclusions.

Your mission statement is your constitution and creed, written in the affirmative. No rule says it has to be a particular length. Simply, it must speak to you, creating energy, excitement, and enthusiasm that enable you to *Want It! Create It! Live It!*

You need mission statements for your business and your personal life. You'll find that each is different and there is harmony between them. If what you want for your personal life is contradicted by your business mission, your ladder of success is leaning on the wrong wall!

Here is Empower U's mission statement:

203

Empower U Mission Statement

To continually build quality relationships that allow our clients to reach their Potential. To Train, Coach and Facilitate the most Powerful Leadership Training this world has ever experienced. We are committed to do this and bring Passion, Enthusiasm, and Focus to our Families, Communities, Businesses, and the World.

We commit to assist our team members in being their dreams by doing the following:

WANT IT — We will foster an environment of continual improvement. This "Culture" of creative discontent will stir our clients—both internal and external—with a Passion to continually challenge themselves and others to be the "Best of the Best."

CREATE IT — We will continue to lead by example and dream BIG, to shoot for the moon, to create a future that honors who we are and what we do. We will never accept *good nuff* and we will live with the idea that "We can do better!" This will be done with an enthusiastic attitude and a humble spirit, accepting the responsibility of being the individuals and the organization "that we could have been."

LIVE IT — We commit to be unlike most other training organizations and "Walk Our Talk." Our tag line of "Leadership in Motion" will be an expression of our lives as an organization, as well as the unique individuals that we all are, independent of each other. We will know that we are making the world a bit better as we live our lives with a noble cause. The world will be a better place tomorrow because **Empower U** was here today!

We commit to do all these things with...
Passion—Heart, Body, and Soul.

CHAPTER 9: PURPOSE!

Creating your mission statement is an opportunity to be the architect of your life and create the organization or life you want.

Think of your mission statement as a compass that is always true, not changeable like a map. In your journey, you'll need to check your compass often to see if you're still on course. This compass, your mission statement, allows you to get back on course if you wander.

A mission statement for your company keeps you and your team emotionally involved with what you do. It declares who you are, what you do, and the quality in which you do it. It is inspirational, motivational and directional. It allows team members to understand the purpose of the organization and know where they fit in.

Be careful not to confuse your mission with your goals. Goals can be stepping stones to your mission, a very important part of the *how*. Goals are short-term; a mission is long-term. Your mission statement is your creed. It's your shield. It's noble.

How do you create a mission statement? While this is not a 20-minute fill-in-the-blanks process, here are some steps to get your creative energy moving in the right direction. Since this is your *life* we're dealing with, you should spend more than 20 minutes creating the best outcome!

EXERCISE #8

Begin by answering the questions below. Go somewhere you will not be disturbed, where you can play relaxing instrumental music in the background, where you can think clearly without interruptions. Spend five minutes on each question, and put down as many answers as possible for each question:

1. **What are your values?** In other words, what do you want to be the underlying attitude in the way you do business—the ideal business culture? What's important to you? Integrity, compassion, teamwork, passion, enthusiasm? List all the values that are important to you. Make sure you think and write for the entire five minutes. If you run out of ideas and words, push yourself to think of even more!

2. **What are your roles?** What are the different roles your company plays to its internal and external clients? Coach, trainer, assistant buyer, dream-builder...? Again push yourself for the entire 5 minutes.

3. **Why do you do what you do?** I'm not thinking about profit, products or services. What's a deeper reason? (Xerox doesn't make

copiers; they improve office productivity. Empower U doesn't train people to be more effective; we help them reignite Passion that drives and improves the quality of their relationships, both personal and professional.) Get emotionally involved with your mission, and dig deep.

NOTES TO MYSELF

Before you go any further, get out your writing paper again and answer these questions.

After you have answered these questions, go through all three lists, circling the top answers in each category. These nine answers best describe how you feel, and you have an excellent basis for a powerful mission statement.

Circle your top three answers in all three categories now. Then gather the nine responses together on a clean sheet of paper.

Once you've transferred these responses to a clean sheet of paper, formulate them into a two–to–three-sentence statement that flows from your heart, stating who you are, what you do, and the quality in which you do it. If you are the leader of a team, get them participating. Without involvement there is no commitment.

BECOMING YOUR DREAMS

You still need your own personal mission statement but, if you start with your company's or department's mission statement, you and your clients will be well served by including your team in the thinking process.

As you work, three questions will tell you if your mission statement is on target:

1. **Does it describe the best possible you?**
2. **Does it list the principles you want you and your organization to live by?**
3. **Does it inspire you?**

Answer these questions honestly and you'll know how well you've done. Of course, you can always do better. Your mission statement will continue to evolve and clarify itself.

Once the statement is in a form that speaks to you, type it up, or write it in calligraphy, or color it. Do something to convey its importance in your life, and then make copies to post everywhere you spend more than 10 minutes a day!

Ensure that you're held accountable to live your mission statement by giving copies to your friends, family, and coworkers. This will allow them to support and encourage you.

Post it everywhere—make sure you can see your compass and your map—so your mind sees and thinks about your mission all the time. Give your RAS something to focus on.

Apply CANI

People who continue to make a difference never feel they've done *everything* to fulfill their Purpose. That's the message of CANI—Constant And Never-Ending Improvement. Or, as we say it at Empower U, "Is your sign 'Under Construction'?"

EXERCISE #9

The two charts at the end of this chapter are provided to help you develop the CANI/"Under Construction" habit regarding your mission.

On the first chart, describe ways your mission fills a need and how you are fulfilling your Purpose—what is different because you understand *why* you're here.

In Chapter 3, you answered 9 of 11 questions:

1. What qualities do I want to have in my life?
2. How am I reinforcing these values?
3. From which roles in my life do I find the most personal satisfaction?
4. What do I like most about the work I do?
5. What do I like least about my work?
6. How can I change the things I like least?
7. What are my business' visible beliefs?
8. What would be the ideal culture for my business?

BECOMING YOUR DREAMS

9. How does the current business culture compare to my ideal culture?

Once you've completed the first chart, you'll use the second chart to focus on meeting your CANI goal. I told you we would answer two more questions later, and later is now:

10. In what specific ways am I progressing toward my Vision, honoring my Purpose?
11. Am I doing everything I can to walk my talk and close the gap between what is and what can be in my life?

Answer the second chart's questions with these outcomes in mind:

- *How am I moving toward my ideal and becoming my dreams?*

- *How can I close the gap between what is and what could be? As a leader, what more can I do to Live It?*

You and I are here for a reason, and when you live your life like it matters, it does.

Purpose: it's what leaders pursue.

WAYS I AM MAKING A DIFFERENCE:

MY MISSION IS:

HOW AM I MOVING TOWARD MY IDEAL?

HOW CAN I CLOSE THE GAP?

CHAPTER 9: **PURPOSE!**

The Next Right Thing

Working with Passion, committed to the cause
Doing God's work behind the eight ball...no time to pause.
Good times or bad, sure that this is my calling,
Running uphill just to keep from falling.
Work all day, maybe seven or eight—
My death to sleep—carrying the world's heavy freight.
The Next Right Thing, this is what to do.
Next right for What? When? ...and for Who?

I am tired of fighting to swallow little water
So many changes—I will be a good father.
Emotions are jumbled. They go up...go down.
I don't want to hurt others—my actions bring frowns.
This hole I dug, happened with unconscious competence.
Taking care of one person at another's expense.
The Next Right Thing, this is what I should do
Next right for What? When? ... and for Who?

People jump ship—short journey left scars
Wanted to make all happy, stuck behind limiting bars.
I owe this and am responsible for that...
Form one long line and let's draw from a hat.
Frustrated with the circumstance, bitten with disappointment.
Some think I am Satan's child, others withhold judgment.
The Next Right Thing, this is what I want to do
Next right for What? When? ...and for Who?

I am doing the right thing...I am...I think
Right for who...it changes with a blink!
Take care of this at the others expense
Working to be congruent, to some makes no sense.
Some look for reasons to believe, some for reasons to not
I give both ammo, some can be a dead shot.
The Next Right Thing, this is what I will do
Next right for What? When? ... Next right for Who?

Scott V. Black

BECOMING YOUR DREAMS

The word "lead," at its root, means "go, travel, guide."
Leadership has about it a kinesthetic feel, a sense of
movement. Leaders "go first." They're pioneers.
They begin the quest for a new order. They
venture into unexplored territory
and guide us to new and
unfamiliar destinations.
In contrast, the root origin of "manage" is a word
meaning "hand." At its core, managing is about
"handling" things, about maintaining order,
about organization and control.
The critical difference between management and
leadership is reflected in the root meanings of
the two words—the difference between what
it means to handle things and what it means
to go places. The unique role of leaders
is to take us to places we've
never been before.

— Kouzes and Postner
The Leadership Challenge

CHAPTER 10:
4 Cs OF LEADERSHIP!

The talents, experiences, and personalities of successful leaders vary widely. Some have a "full-speed ahead" approach. Other leaders are more cautious, subdued, analytical. Daniel Goleman, author of *Emotional Intelligence* and cochair of Rutgers University's Consortium for Research on Emotional Intelligence in Organizations, reports that different situations require different leadership styles. For instance, he says mergers often need the leadership of a *sensitive negotiator,* while turnarounds usually require a *forceful authority* style.

However, in every situation studied by the Consortium, the hallmark of successful leadership has been *emotional intelligence.* Goleman says the components of this quality are:

- self-awareness
- self-regulation
- motivation
- empathy
- social skill

BECOMING YOUR DREAMS

Let me prove my case: Many companies use competency models (identifying what leaders do well) to spot, train, and promote effective leadership candidates. In a study of competency models, Goleman grouped leaders' personal capabilities into three categories:

- *technical* skills, like accounting and business planning
- *cognitive* skills, like analysis and reasoning
- *emotional intelligence,* like abilities to work with others and lead change

Cognitive skills (seeing the big picture and creating a long-term Vision) were found to be especially important. However, in calculating the ratio of technical skills, intellectual skills, and emotional intelligence as factors in excellent performance, Goleman's study proves emotional intelligence is *twice* as important as the other factors for jobs at all levels.

Even more interesting, his analysis shows that emotional intelligence plays an *increasingly important role in a company's highest levels,* where differences in technical skills become less and less important. And, when comparing one senior leader to another, nearly 90% of the difference in their effectiveness was attributed to leaders' *emotional intelligence* factors, rather than their cognitive skills, reasoning, or brain power.

5 FACTORS OF EMOTIONAL INTELLIGENCE:

- **Self-Awareness** Ability to recognize and understand their own moods, emotions, and drives—and how these affect others.
  Demonstrated by self-confidence, realistic self-assessment, self-deprecating sense of humor.

- **Self-Regulation** Ability to control or redirect disruptive impulses or moods; self-discipline—tendency to think before acting and suspend prejudgment.
  Demonstrated by integrity and trustworthiness, comfort with uncertainty, openness to change.

- **Motivation** Passion for work beyond reasons of money or status; tendency to pursue achievement with energy and persistence.
  Demonstrated by strong drive to set and reach goals, optimism in failure, commitment to the organization.

- **Empathy** Ability to understand the emotional composition (needs, perceptions, and responses) of others; skill in responding to people according to their emotional reactions.
  Demonstrated by expertise in building and retaining talents of others, cross-cultural sensitivity, service to clients and customers.

- **Social Skill** Practical ability to manage relationships and build cooperative networks; finding common ground and establishing rapport.
  Demonstrated by affecting change, gaining consensus; persuasiveness, endorsement; expertise in building and leading teams.

adapted from Harvard Business Review, November–December 1998

Of course, leaders still need intellectual and technical ability, but in the "old days" of leadership, these skills were overemphasized and the qualities that comprise emotional intelligence were largely ignored. The good news of Goleman's studies confirms that emotional intelligence can be learned! It's not easy, because it requires time, practice, experience, error, correction, and—most of all—the critical key of Commitment.

When you think about key leaders in your life, what qualities of their leadership do you admire most? Aren't they the Lou Holtz-type people-skills we considered in Chapter 7: trust, commitment, and care? To bring this home in a tangible way, complete **EXERCISE #10** on the following page. As simple as it seems, don't skip it. Spend a few minutes thinking about the person who has had the strongest impact for good on your life—the individual who, in large part, shaped you into who you are today because of his or her leadership. Then, answer these questions:

1. **What are the qualities I admire most about this person?**
2. **What are the traits and qualities I have gained from this person?**
3. **What are the "ripple effects" that have shown up in my life because of this leader's impact?**

THE LEADER IN MY LIFE:

MY LEADER'S NAME IS: _____

The qualities I most admire: _____

_____

_____

_____

_____

_____

_____

_____

Traits and qualities I've gained: _____

_____

_____

_____

_____

_____

_____

_____

_____

Ripple effects in my life: _____

_____

_____

_____

_____

_____

_____

_____

Before we move on, look back on the qualities and traits you most admire and have gained
from this leader. Divide them into two categories: Attitude and Skill. Mark an "A" on qualities
that are mostly attitudinal. Then go back and
mark an "S" on those that are mostly skill. You
might have listed several with "A/S" but you'll
probably find a majority of them are based in
your leader's attitudes. True leaders demonstrate
Emotional Intelligence by controlling their
attitude.

4 Cs of leadership

When you live your life like it matters, it
does. When you live with this *intentionality,*
you affect others' lives in the same sense that
the leader in your life impacted you. Your life
has at least as much potential for influence as
the leader you just described! In order to get
to this level, let me introduce you to the 4 Cs
of Leadership:

- Commitment
- Communication
- Clear Vision
- Consensus

The one word I always use when talking
about Commitment is trust. Trust and Commitment go hand-in-hand. How can someone

commit to you without trusting you? Without Commitment, nothing great can be reached or sustained.

So the first C on this list is Commitment. We've dedicated an entire chapter to this quality. We've quoted Lou Holtz and thought about trustworthiness. When you followed a leader to the point that this individual made a significant difference in your life, you showed great trust in his or her Commitment.

What are you hearing and saying?

The second C is Communication. Whenever we talk about Communication, we must consider:

1.   The Communication we have with others.
2.   The Communication we have with ourselves.

Communication is the foundation for all relationships, both business and personal. When you improve Communication, you improve relationships. What good is your mission, vision, values and beliefs if they go uncommunicated to others? We can't be effective leaders if we don't communicate effectively.

Year after year, senior executives are surveyed to determine which business skill is most valuable. Despite new trends and concepts *du jour,* Communication always tops the list. The "right answer" does no good unless it is shared.

BECOMING YOUR DREAMS

Be aware of how you communicate with *yourself* too. We wouldn't let others talk to us in the ways we talk to ourselves! Some of us have a CD playing in our heads that doesn't support our desire to be Best of the Best. Some of us have been playing negative messages so long, that they're on an 8-track tape! It's time to become the Steven Spielberg of your life—*leave some stuff on the cutting room floor!*

If your self-talk keeps telling you that you're a failure, realize that this negative feedback has been working perfectly to keep you living and working at a lower level.

If you don't like that result, change your approach. Play better messages to get better results. As I said before, insanity is doing the same thing over and over but expecting to get different results—that's why they call it crazy! Change your internal conversations to support becoming "The Best Possible You."

This technique has been used by legendary basketball coach John Wooden. In his book *Wooden: A Lifetime of Observations and Reflection On and Off the Court,* he wrote that one of his greatest strengths has been his ability to keep out negative thoughts. He didn't say his greatest strength was his players or UCLA or his coaches! His self-communication influenced how he felt about all of those because it first determined how he felt about himself.

We spent a lot of time earlier on the ways we speak to others. In addition to the negative things we say and hear from ourselves, we can too readily say negative things to others and hear negative in others' comments to us. True leaders are approachable and do not say things that build barriers between people.

To be effective, Communication requires two smaller Cs, as well. We need to be:

- clear
- concise

This means saying what we mean and meaning what we say. It means using our words to create a sharply focused picture of what we want.

Get a BHAG

The third C stands for Clear Vision. (Again, we've devoted an entire chapter to Vision.) Leaders *clarify* their Vision continually by asking:

1. Where are we now?
2. Where are we going?
3. What will it take to get there and how long?

Leaders have *BHAGs*—Big Hairy Audacious Goals (a term from James C. Collins' book, *Built*

BECOMING YOUR DREAMS

to Last: Successful Habits of Visionary Companies). Leaders' Vision always exceeds their grasp, so they must stretch and grow. They understand that they can't create in real life what they can't create in their mind's eye, in their imagination. (Remember, because people want to be a part of something bigger than themselves, a visionary leader with BHAGs can fulfill this need and desire.)

Yes, leaders have Vision—they're dreamers. But the operative term is *Clear* Vision. It's not enough just to "see" that there's something better out there. Leaders' BHAGs are definite. They know what their goals will look like, smell, sound, taste, and feel like when achieved. Leaders' plans may be written in sand, but their goals are set firmly in concrete—methods may change, but outcomes are assured. Their success isn't based on guesswork and good wishes; it is founded on clear Vision and clear Communication that gains clear Commitment.

In our *Leadership Adventure* class, sighted students guide blindfolded students up and over, down and under, barriers! We do this so the person with sight learns to portray a Clear Vision of their surroundings. Because there is clarity in Vision and Communication, students being led are able to trust and make clear Commitment to their leaders.

224

All together now

Once you have Commitment and your Communication is congruent with the Clear Vision you have established, it's time to solidify your team through Consensus.

Consensus is gaining agreement in groups for problem-solving and decision making. In this process, everyone discusses issues and reaches decisions that all can agree to support. Consensus incorporates the knowledge, experience, feeling, and ideas of the group. It causes team members to buy in. It's taking time to reach agreement, even if that's not something you really want to do. It's not dictating or negotiating. And it's the fourth C because Consensus is almost impossible before achieving Commitment, Communication, and Clear Vision.

Within yourself, agreement with your words and actions concerning personal goals and ambitions is called *congruence*. When your words and actions are congruent, you've achieved personal Consensus.

As a boss, you may be able to dictate direction to your team without Consensus. You can mandate and manipulate, but will this method accomplish what you want? If you want only to be The Boss, this tactic may work temporarily. But if you want to be a leader of people who are committed to the team and its cause, your ability to build Consensus will determine if you can get what you want.

In Chris' book, *Getting to Know You,* he wrote that finesse is stronger than force. In the long run, it takes less energy to encourage co-operation than it does to enforce compliance. With the former, you work with willing hearts; with the latter, you compel unwilling hands.

Challenge or change

Our *Leadership Awakening* and *Leadership Adventure* classes create some of the most challenging and powerful experiences anyone will ever encounter.

In *The Leadership Experience Part I: Leadership Awakening,* participants learn about 100% Commitment to start living to their potential. When everyone in the group makes that Commitment, an incredible team is formed. They learn the *Want It! Create It! Live It!* concept and *live* the six words of Passion, Focus, Commitment, Team, Vision, and Purpose.

In *Part II: Leadership Adventure,* participants figure out how they fit into a team and see what a real team can accomplish. They trust each other with their lives, relying on the 4 Cs of Leadership.

CHAPTER 10: 4 Cs OF LEADERSHIP!

While reading a book isn't a substitute for living *The Leadership Experience,* I hope working your way through *Becoming Your Dreams* has been a challenging experience for you. More than that, I want it to be life-*changing.*

This book is about *leadership* training, not *management* training. It's about gaining control of your destiny by becoming the leader of your own life today. When you develop Passion, Focus, Commitment, Team, Vision, and Purpose for yourself, you'll find you're equipped to discover and instill it in others. You'll become a *developer* of people, a *builder* of dreams, a true *leader* of people who live purposefully and enthusiastically...Heart, Body, and Soul.

To become this kind of leader, you and I must be willing to accept the possibility that maybe—just maybe—we're not perfect; that maybe, there's room for improvement. Maybe we can be better at everything we do in our lives: a better team leader, sales manager, spouse, parent, member of our community and religion.

If, while reading this book, you haven't challenged yourself to raise the bar in your own life, ask yourself, *Why not? Where else in my life— when given opportunities to truly push and stretch myself, to step over the line and work to become*

the Best of the Best—where else in my life do I
not take advantage of such opportunities?"

Some of the exercises in this book have
made people turn and run, but it seems you
have chosen to stay, to trust the process, to
complete your assignments...and for this, I commend you. But now you have a new challenge:
you must continue to raise your own bar! The
Time Is Now...to Live It!

It will be easy to forget your experiences
in this book and fall back, because old patterns
pull at each of us. So don't permit these ideas
to present a one-time challenge. Within the next
30 days, read again what you wrote in the exercises and notes, and the commitments you made
to yourself.

It's taken you a lot of work to get this far,
while it would have taken none to avoid the dis-
comfort of self-examination and personal growth.
After all, it takes no effort to remain at the bottom of a crab bucket! Just as there are crabs in
the bucket that pull others down, the disillu-
sionment of false Belief Systems and unhealthy
habits await you when you close this book.

To counteract this, remember what you've
learned and experienced. Notice that you really
are responding differently to people, hearing
things you haven't heard before, seeing life with

"eyes" you haven't used before.

Your own experience of *sensory acuity* (becoming truly aware of how unaware you've been...up until now) will cause you to listen, and not just hear. When you work with people, your heart will be warmed in a way it was never warmed before, and you'll have a choice to make:

Will you forget what you've learned and slip back down into the crab bucket? Or will you keep struggling to escape the bucket, reaching toward a life that matters?

The truth is, you will expend at least as much energy in running away from life as you will in stretching out to grab it.

You see, my friend, once you know the truth, *you're ruined for life!* There's no excuse for returning to what used to be *good nuff*. You've written your eulogy; you know how you want to finish. Unless you now turn your pretty words into actions, then "pretty in a box" is the best you can hope for.

The power of perhaps

I close some of my speeches with the story of an old man who lived in an isolated Chinese village hundreds of years ago. It was a very poor community, but because he had both a horse and a son, he was considered very fortunate.

One day, the man's horse ran away, and the

villagers came to comfort him. They said, "You are the most *unfortunate* of all men, because your horse has run away." The old man simply looked at them and said, "Perhaps."

A while later, the old man's missing horse returned, bringing three wild horses with it. The other villagers came to celebrate and said, "You are the most *fortunate* of all men, because now you have four horses." The old man looked at them and said, "Perhaps."

Later, the old man's son was training one of the horses when he was thrown off and shattered his leg. The villagers returned again to console him. "You are the most *unfortunate* of all men, for now your only son is crippled." And the old man simply said, "Perhaps."

Then a War Lord invaded the village, carrying off all the able-bodied young men to fight the invading Huns. When only his son was left behind because of his broken leg, the villagers gathered around the old man and said, "You are the most *fortunate* of all men, because your son has been spared from battle." And the old man said, "Perhaps...."

What does this story have to do with my speech or this book? What you do with your life, from this moment, is a *perhaps*.

Perhaps you really can live your life the

way you want it. Yes, you're free to ask, "But what if Scott's principles *won't* work for me?" Maybe you should ask instead, "What if they *will* work for me?"

You can find an excuse through negative self-talk: "What if this whole thing is just hype? What if it does work for some people, but it doesn't for my situation?"

Well, I have a "Chinese Challenge" for you: *Perhaps...Maybe...Why not...What if it did?*

What do you want?

You've got little to lose and so much to gain. Consider how much life may open up to you when you live your life—not by the *odds against* your success but by the *possibilities for* your success!

So...Passion. Focus. Commitment. Team. Vision. Purpose. These six words matter in your work, your life, your world. They have framed everything that happened as you read this book. They are the tools you use to become your dreams—they are how you *Want it! Create it! Live it!*

What do you want? And do you want it so much that you'll push through self-imposed barriers and knock down your walls? Do you want it enough to pick yourself up, dust yourself off, and hit it again and again and again—or are you just a *wannabe?* If you really *Want It*, then you'll step over the line and *Create It!*

You have creative work to do. Is your legacy in place? Have you created your future? Have you left a lasting mark? When you live your life like it matters, it does. It's hard to live a life worth celebrating without dreams and Vision. If you stop at *Want It*, you will be just a dreamer. To fulfill your dreams, you must step over the line and *Create It!*

Then, every day, you must *Live It!* Walk your talk. Be congruent in your words and actions. Defend your life against the dream stealers. Be an example of a life worth living. Show others that every day is a great day to be alive. You'll become the leader you were born to be because people are looking for someone or something to follow. Teach them to follow truth and life.

Benediction

I hope you'll tell people what a wonderful book you've read—*please!*—and tell them you're going to change your world by changing your life. Just know they're going to tell you why it won't work. They'll belittle your ambitions and ask if you "drank the Kool-Aid." Don't take it personally and don't get angry with them. It's just their fear of the unknown speaking.

Instead, do this: forget your speeches and determined declarations to make a difference. What you do speaks louder than what you say anyway. Just live your life like it matters, and show people through your actions that your life—and theirs too—is worth living.

Become your dreams! Do it with Passion...Heart, Body, and Soul!

focus • passion • purpose • team • vision • commitment • focus • passion

heart
body
soul

WANT IT. CREATE IT. LIVE IT.

About
Scott V. Black

Scott V. Black is CEO of Empower U, Inc., which he founded in 1994. He is certified as a Human Behavioral Specialist and a Master Practitioner of Neurolinguistic Programming (NLP), working with clients to help them obtain personal and professional goals. He has worked with executives at Coca-Cola, Nabisco, Kraft, CompuCom, American Athletic, Cintas: The Uniform Company, Michelin, Baylor Health Care Foundation, Cingular Wireless, Army National Guard, and other companies across North America.

Scott is a professional member of the National Speakers Association. He is an accomplished speaker, author, songwriter, and poet, and he has some singing credits to his name. He is also credited as a writer and producer of the musical CD, *Awakening*. His two-part leadership development program, *The Leadership Experience*, consists of *Leadership Awakening* and *Leadership Adventure*. It is gaining a national reputation as the most powerful leadership training available today.

Scott's strong belief in the potential of the human being motivates his passion to train and coach business leaders and their teams to be the "Best of the Best." He is an inspiring leader and motivator, committed to empowering individuals to live with Passion—Heart, Body, and Soul.

Scott V. Black lives with his two children, Faith and Christian, at the HBS Fernley Ranch outside of Reno, Nevada. He is available for keynote addresses, custom training, and personal coaching worldwide. He can be reached through his corporate website: www.empoweru.net.

The Ultimate Leadership Experience
PART I: LEADERSHIP AWAKENING

Leadership Awakening is Part I of the Ultimate Leadership Experience. Everything you have ever read, believed, or thought about leadership will come alive in this 2½-day intense journey. It's about pushing ourselves and others to be Best of the Best. To start reaching our potential...to realize that no matter how well we are doing, we can always do better...to never again accept "good enough" from ourselves and inspire others to do the same. Experience the ultimate challenge, and awaken to the possibilities. *Leadership Awakening* is a must for anyone who calls himself or herself a leader or has a desire to lead.

As a result of attending Empower U's *Leadership Awakening* workshop, you will:

- Speak with power, authority, and conviction while gaining agreement
- Analyze strengths and weaknesses in relation to your leadership skills, and make necessary improvements
- Identify and implement your Mission and Vision
- Develop effective and precise communication that inspires and motivates others
- Enhance decision-making skills and ability to take action when necessary
- Discover ability to tackle any challenge while staying focused and committed
- Develop greater loyalty and dedication among coworkers
- Build and develop stronger, more powerful, more effective teams
- Focus more precisely on the mission of the organization and stay "On Purpose"
- Take charge, lead with Commitment, Focus, and increase Passion
- Develop motivational skills
- Develop a greater level of Enthusiasm and Passion within the organization

Resulting in a direct bottom-line increase in effective leadership abilities, productivity, and profitability for the company.

The Ultimate Leadership Experience
PART II: HBS LEADERSHIP ADVENTURE

HBS Leadership Adventure is Part II of the Ultimate Leadership Experience. It takes everything your learned in *Leadership Awakening* and puts it into motion! Through an outdoor weekend at the beautiful 400-acre LDL Ranch, 70 miles southeast of San Diego, California, you will be presented with challenging obstacles where you, as a team, must come together to accomplish tasks as they arise. The team actually runs the classes, focusing on team building and honing leadership skills in an experiential environment.

As a result of attending Empower U's *Leadership Adventure* workshop, you will:

- Practice and master the 4 Cs of Leadership
- Gain skills to build consensus within a group
- Strengthen communication skills
- Experience the power of commitment within a team
- Pinpoint personality strengths and weaknesses to develop a high-performance team
- Clarify your vision
- Learn how to push past conflict and come together as a team
- Build and develop stronger, more powerful, more effective teams
- Capitalize on your team's greatest strengths and compensate for weaknesses

On a scale of 1–100, *Leadership Awakening* takes participants from level 1 to level 25. *HBS Leadership Adventure* takes participants from level 26 to 100 and beyond, learning to work and win with Passion...Heart, Body, and Soul.

Prerequisite: *Leadership Awakening* (Part I of the Ultimate Leadership Experience)

EQ: COMMUNICATING WITH POWER

Communication is the foundation for all relationships in our personal and professional lives. *EQ: Communicating with Power* deals with the two types of communication that take place in our lives:

Communication with others

Virtually every survey of senior executives reveals that effective communication is the most important business skill. No one can be persuasive, manage well, lead others, participate cooperatively, affect change, or build strong relationships without the ability to communicate effectively.

Communication with ourselves

The personal dialogue that occurs inside us is ongoing, and it is the foundation for how we see most things in life, how we interpret what we see, and what others do to us. Neurolinguistic Programming (NLP)) teaches that each individual processes information primarily in one of three ways: *visually* (by sight or seeing), *auditorially* (by language or sounds), and *kinesthetically*, by experience or emotion). In *EQ*, you will learn to identify these three modes, discover how each processes information, and gain ability to identify the styles in others.

EQ also explores how human behavior can be categorized across four primary dimensions of *Dominance, Influence, Stability,* and *Compliance*, using tools based on 70 years of research in predictive behavior. Emotional Intelligence is the ability to tune in to feelings, senses, appraisals, actions, and intentions, so we can guide our behavior and better solve problems, resolving conflicts, and becoming more self-motivated. As a result of attending EQ, you will:

- Improve and enhance communication skills
- Better understand self and others
- Foster greater teamwork
- Manage and lead more effectively
- Discover and value strengths of self and others
- Increase your capacity for influence, sales, and productivity
- Reduce conflict and stress

POWER GOAL SETTING

Setting goals is a familiar activity, but *getting* goals is foreign to many. *Power Goal Setting* is about learning how to reach your goals.

As a participant in this 4-hour program, you will learn some very powerful *focusing techniques* along with state-of-the-art goal setting skills. Through a series of processes, you will push yourself to get in touch with what you really want. You'll master creative visualization or mental rehearsal, because when you can mentally create it, you can achieve it! Author Stephen Covey has called this "beginning with the end in mind."

During the class, we'll cover how the mind works, the power of focus, what true commitment means, and how to "future pace" yourself to accomplish your goals. After this 3½-hour experiential workshop, the entire class moves outdoors to put these newfound skills to the test. Coals from a bonfire are spread over a 16-foot runway, starting at Point A (representing where you are today) and Point B (representing where you will be tomorrow—your goal). As you complete your walk across 1400–1600° coals, you will understand that "If I can do *this*, I can do *anything* I put my mind to!"

Rest assured, we never talk anyone into walking on fire. Truth be known, half the people who sign up for this class think they would really like to learn these powerful focusing and goal setting techniques but have no intention of ever strolling across hot coals. With rare exception, they see the incredible energy and the potential of a focused mind in their friends, who were just as skeptical of completing their walk, and they decide to walk themselves, taking control of their lives and accomplishing their goals!

When an entire project team experiences the firewalk, results for the company are astonishing! The searing coals represent any obstacles that may pop up throughout the project. When the team realizes that it can stay focused on the goal and keep moving forward—no matter what the obstacles—*goals are achieved!*

Read what our "Raving Fans" have to say about the Leadership Experience

I have attended literally hundreds of seminars and training programs that were intended to develop my leadership skills, most of which long ago faded from my memory. Your program, however, is one that I know will be a part me for the rest of my life. —*Glenn Box*
Coca-Cola Enterprises

What an experience! It was an incredible, exciting, challenging, up-lifting and rewarding weekend—seeing a group of strangers from all walks of life come together as a team in less than 48 hours. This is exactly what you call it: an *Awakening!* I have a new passion for life, a deeper love for my family, a new focus in my work, and a heartfelt respect for all that I come in contact with. For this I am grateful.
—*Jeff Grove*
Zone Business Manager
Frito Lay, Inc.

Over the years, I've had the opportunity to attend many well known courses that concentrate on personal and interpersonal development, leadership, and management skills. Your training is different! Through intense participation, your course has helped me to see the world through an entirely new frame of reference. The bar is now being raised daily at Tony's Fine Foods, to the benefit of our customers, suppliers and employees. —*Scott Berger*
CEO, Tony's Fine Foods

I must tell you, not once in my life have I experienced this kind of training. It has already made an impact on my personal and profes-sional life. This past weekend was leadership at its best. I definitely recommend your training to anyone who's a leader or who wants to become one. I promise, those who commit to this class will thank them-selves for doing so. I know—I'm one of them! —*Adam L. Padilla*
Director of Marketing/Coupon Operations
Texas Food Industry Association

READ WHAT OUR "RAVING FANS" HAVE TO SAY ABOUT
THE LEADERSHIP EXPERIENCE

Congratulations on having such a powerful program to offer to everyone! The *Leadership Awakening* program is really beyond my wildest expectations. It is second to none! After graduating, I now have commitment and focus in all aspects of my life. The best part is that I have courage to break down any walls to achieve my goals! After working with Empower U, our employees have purpose, vision, focus, commitment and the courage to never accept "good nuff" again! Thank you again for such a powerful program.   —*Debbie Oster*
Director of Human Resources, Coca-Cola
Western Canada Division

My time at Empower U was like "Dale Carnegie on Acid!" Your staff taught me how to "turbocharge my Franklin Covey!" I was fortunate to be number six from our company, and my brother, Eric and I have already committed to sending you twelve more of our core covenant.
—*Greg J. Stille*
Vice President: Nugget Markets, Inc.

This experience reinforced fundamental concepts and values that I believed, but up until now I had not clearly brought into focus. As other colleagues have this experience, our workplace will undergo a profound change. I have participated in many civilian personal and professional development programs, such as: Increasing Human Effectiveness, The Seven Habits..., Investment in Excellence, Interpersonal Management Skills, Strength Deployment Inventory, and Myers/Briggs, to name a few. These programs have their merits. However, none matches the power or passion of *Leadership Awakening*. I have undertaken extensive military training over the past 15 years, and *Leadership Awakening* is commensurate with some of the best! I look forward with anticipation to *Leadership Adventure!*
—*Walter J. Moore*
Army National Guard of the United States

"Incredible" is the first word that comes to mind. *Leadership Awakening* has changed my life. I now live life with passion—heart, body, and soul—every day of my life. This class enabled me to look inside and realize the power of the mind and the soul. One process allowed me to look at the end of my life and understand and identify how I was living in the present. I want everyone in the world to have the opportunity to experience this life-changing course. —*Jason Nichols*
Coca-Cola Enterprises: North Texas Division

READ WHAT OUR "RAVING FANS" HAVE TO SAY ABOUT
THE LEADERSHIP EXPERIENCE

My family and business colleagues notice the change, seeing a side of me that even I didn't know existed. I am able to share purpose, commitment and focus with my business associates, resulting in improved performance and teamwork in just the past week. It is amazing how quickly "try" and "good enough" have become unacceptable in discussions of meeting commitments. Personally, my family is seeing a positive change in my attitude and focus on their needs and in my passionate involvement in their lives. I'm scheduling my wife to attend *Leadership Awakening* very soon, and the entire Senior Management Team of CompuCom will attend before the end of May.

—*Anthony Pellegrini*
Senior Vice President, Sales, CompuCom

Let me say that coming from the point of view of a professional trainer and communicator myself, your program is awesome! Your methods work! My family and business associates have already commented on the difference. And I've enjoyed my renewed ability to focus and commit with passion, purpose and vision! Keep up the good fight, and I will continue to sing your praises.   —*Jeff Justice*
"Humor" Resources Director

I am a decorated combat veteran of Viet Nam and spent 20 years in the US Army, half of those years with the Special Operations Forces at Ft. Bragg, NC. I know a thing or two about leadership and motivation, but *Leadership Awakening* taught me some new things—about myself, my relationships, and my abilities. So I say to Empower U: As a veteran, I salute you; as a leader, I commend you; and as a human being, I thank you.   —*Ron Chewning*
Regional Sales Director, Strategic Accounts Gulf States
Cingular Wireless

As a golf professional, I am constantly searching for ways, other than daily physical practice, to improve my golf game. My hope, prior to this class, was to have a good time and bring back some leadership skills I could apply to my everyday work habits, making myself a better leader for my staff. What I came away with was not only that, but also commitment. Thank you again for the most inspirational and useful two and a half days I have ever spent to simply make me a better man. I am truly a leader who has been awakened!

—*Scott Sawyer, PGA*
Head Golf Professional, Mira Vista Golf Club

READ WHAT OUR "RAVING FANS" HAVE TO SAY ABOUT
THE LEADERSHIP EXPERIENCE

Wow—what an incredible experience! To say that the *Leadership Awakening* class I just completed exceeded my expectations would be a tremendous understatement. Over the past twenty years, I have spent literally thousands of dollars on various training classes, seminars, tapes and books. I can honestly say that just two days of *Leadership Awakening* taught me more than all those previous materials combined. It is truly something to be experienced!

—Jeff Bramble
President
American Athletic, Inc.

My job as Training and Development Manager with the Champaign Police is to find the most current and applicable training for every employee. There are numerous "management" courses for Law Enforcement available, but I was looking for a Leadership course to help our managers develop into the leaders that are needed in these changing times we live in. What I experienced in the *Leadership Awakening* course was nothing short of amazing! Your class is exactly what I was looking for, not only for my department, but also for my family, my community, and myself. I am recommending that every manager in our department attend the *Leadership Awakening* class to help them find their mission in life and their careers. What a blessing for a leader to have an entire team focused on achieving the goals of the department!

—Lt. Michael Paulus
Training & Development Manager
Champaign, Illinois, Police Department

With over 20 years of military service as an infantry officer, I've had opportunities to attend our nation's most rigorous leadership training courses. Your program measures up to these in every respect. This course is a must for leaders of all types and at all levels. Leadership, as you know, is more than a series of magic words and phrases we apply to specific situations. Your program ensures that we understand and embrace the artist who lies deep within us. If we can do that, we will get more out of our relationships, get more out of the people around us, and get more out of ourselves. I recommend your program to anyone who wants to be a better leader or citizen.

—William Potter
Lieutenant Colonel, MTARNG
Commanding (RRM)

READ WHAT OUR "RAVING FANS" HAVE TO SAY ABOUT
THE LEADERSHIP EXPERIENCE

I am still buzzing over my Empower U and *Leadership Awakening* experience. As a sales and sales-training professional for over 20 years, I thought I'd heard of or attended everything out there on leadership and/or maximized productivity. How wrong I was!

—Eric Harmon
CEO/President, Resource Development Group

In my 28 years of tenure with Coca-Cola in Western Canada, I can truly say that this is, without question, the best training I've received—including a variety of very good programs that I have been fortunate to participate in throughout the years. *—Len Jordan*
Coca-Cola Bottling Company
Western Canada Division

Empower U was an extremely powerful experience and clearly one of the best training and personal development courses I have taken since my graduation from the Untied States Military Academy at West Point. I have attended and "suffered" through many management training and so-called leadership development courses based on highly philosophical theories and paradigm shifts. Until Empower U, no training remotely measured up to the level of intensity and full commitment of my West Point experience. Empower U truly challenged and allowed me to "raise the bar" higher than I have in the past several years of my professional and personal life. *—Kevin B. Wilson*
Regional Director, Strategic Accounts
Cingular Wireless

It would be an understatement to say the impact of *Leadership Awakening* is profound. This is the most fulfilling program I have ever experienced. It was unlike anything else, training or otherwise, I have ever undergone. It was intense—as you told us up front—but the effect it has is incredible! I'm a better husband, parent and leader after graduating from *Leadership Awakening*. Your program receives my endorsement—Heart, Body and Soul. My wife is enrolled, my daughter is enrolled in *Teen Awakening,* and many of my colleagues are enrolled. Empower U must flourish and prosper. There are so many people it must touch. Empower U is making the world a better place; you're making a difference. *—Mark Thompson*
General Manager, Northwest Division
Coca-Cola Enterprises

READ WHAT OUR "RAVING FANS" HAVE TO SAY ABOUT
THE LEADERSHIP EXPERIENCE

Knowing what your training did for us at ECR Sales Management 10 years ago, I've committed to again make Empower U Leadership training available to the entire team at POS Sales Management. Thank you for making a difference in my life, my family's, my team's, and so many others that Empower U has touched. —*M.H. "Lefty" Monson*
President, POS Sales Management, Inc.

I already have two of my team members scheduled for the training in the next 30 days, and I am sponsoring my entire organization through your *Leadership Awakening* training. I recommend your training to any business interested in supercharging the effectiveness of their organization. In fact, I recommend your training to everyone, in any walk of life, who seeks to live life more fully. —*Derrel Ness*
President, NSA Distribution

This training encompassed areas that I hadn't even imagined. I recommend Leadership Awakening to anyone who is dedicated to a team approach and looking to breathe new life into a company of any size or age. Its effect is contagiously transferred to all aspects of business life—from company associates to customers to family in general. Empower U staff members conducted themselves in a professional and caring manner, enabling our employees to receive the maximum benefits of their leadership training. We look forward to sending more employees to this powerful leadership training program, continuing our commitment to build a top-notch company and retain employees who are successful and enthusiastic about life and their jobs. The investment we made in your program was worth every penny, and we will reap residual returns for years to come. Thank you for providing this dynamic program to the business community. —*Scott Johnston*
Director of Sales, Posiflex

Thank you so much for your guidance and tenacity, getting us to participate in the Leadership programs you have facilitated for our company. You've made a significant impact on all of us, as well as our business. Over the years, we'd sent a total of 15 team members, including myself, to a combined total of 57 different Leadership and Personal Improvement classes that you were a part of. Our management team offers our sincere gratitude to you and the other team members who were a part of our tremendous growth and profitability. We also thank you as spouses, moms, dads, and grandparents. —*Toby Jensen*
ECR Sales Management, Inc.

READ WHAT OUR "RAVING FANS" HAVE TO SAY ABOUT
THE LEADERSHIP EXPERIENCE

I want to take a couple of minutes to personally thank you and the staff at Empower U for an absolutely awesome weekend adventure at your retreat in San Diego. If *Leadership Awakening* is the "Wake-Up Call to Life," then *Leadership Adventure* is the rocket fuel that will get you there! The biggest thrill I received was attending Adventure with my wife. On a personal level, this has taken a good, solid marriage and made it outstanding. Our communications and expectations of life are both very focused. Empower U's *Leadership Adventure* was the ultimate test to see what kind of leader I thought I was, and the kind of leader I want to become.

—Lonnie Klaich
Director of Finance
St. Mary's Home Care Services

I was at the end of my rope when I came to you for guidance—my team was not communicating. We were in a crisis! I knew from attending *Leadership Awakening* and *Leadership Adventure* that we are all "Under Construction" in our lives. I remembered your discussing another class, *EQ: Communicating with Power,* and knew this was the right time for my team to attend this type of training. What a difference! After just 8 hours in session, we had some repaired relationships, and even laughed some at ourselves. By the end of the class, my team was committed to open communication, rekindling the meaning of "All for one and one for all!" Thank you for giving me and my employees the tools we needed to regain our commitment. Thank you for showing us the different personality types and how we all need each other's unique perspectives to complete the puzzle.

—Mary Anne Kristan
Director, Proposal and Response Center
Cingular Wireless

Thank you for making a difference in my life and the lives of many of our employees and friends. Empower U is not just a seminar about leadership; it's about values, caring, growing, stretching, team building, learning to love others, and learning to love yourself. It gives you the gift of appreciation for life. It enables you to make the wonderful things in your life brighter—and the ability to change things you've always wanted to but never had the guts! I only wish every person on earth had the opportunity to attend Empower U. I can only imagine the better world we would create!

—Rick Reviglio
Western Nevada Supply Company

READ WHAT OUR "RAVING FANS" HAVE TO SAY ABOUT
THE LEADERSHIP EXPERIENCE

I want you to know how much I appreciate the opportunity to attend *Leadership Awakening*. It was by far the most effective and powerful training experience of my life and I thank you for bringing yourself so fully to the work. I've attended several other training sessions that focus on personal mastery—including est, Leadership and Mastery with Peter Senge, The Creating Course developed by Robert Fritz, Creating Results in Organizations with Robert Fritz, Neurolinguistic Programming workshops, and a variety of other therapeutic models during my training in clinical social work. While I've received benefits from each of these, none has been as powerful and life-changing as *Leadership Awakening*. The power in your course pushed me past my own internal barriers and helped me experience the meaning of purpose, commitment, passion and focus. I am bringing these qualities to my work, my life and my relationships.　　　*—Dorothy Weber*
Organization Development Consultant
Intermountain Health Care

Michelin invests heavily in training of all kinds, including team skills training, but very often, we cannot quantify the results of "soft skills training"; we just know that it's the right thing to do. Well, we got a surprise this time! Effective the first day back in the plant:

- The team's quality took an immediate jump worth about $3,000 per week
- Their output took an immediate jump worth about $10,000 per week
- Their attitude took an immediate jump—value...?

Thank you...and well done!　　　*—Doug Cassidy*
Plant Manager, Michelin

How can I put in words on a single sheet of paper everything I've returned with from my *Leadership Awakening* experience? I've had many exciting times in my life, but the emotion and passion totally rivaled what I felt when I married Jill 29 years ago and the births of my two children! I truly realized the awesome power that emotion and passion carry. I have renewed a true sense of happiness, excitement and expectation that I can remember having 30 years ago, fresh out of college and ready to take on the world. There was nothing I couldn't accomplish and—as successful as I've been—I know I will do even more in the time I have left.　　　*—Joe Polich*
Executive Vice President
Production Engine Remanufacturers Association

READ WHAT OUR "RAVING FANS" HAVE TO SAY ABOUT
THE LEADERSHIP EXPERIENCE

The *Leadership Awakening* class is the most impacting, life changing training I have ever attended. I have always been a student of leadership and business principles, and your *Leadership Awakening* training has blown away every book I've ever read and every course I have attended. This training truly enables you to "be as good as you are!"   —*Richard B. Surdykowski, Jr.*
Group Vice President, CINTAS Corporation

Not since my U.S. Army Ranger training have I been pushed to see and feel my ability to live and love life to the fullest. I left your training with a new set of eyes to see what I have been missing, and a new set of ears to hear things that, "up until now," I have not been hearing. Empower U training can teach the oldest dog new definitions of Team, Focus, Purpose, Vision, Commitment, and Passion, using a unique delivery system that must be experienced in order to be understood. I have a fire in me that will last forever, and I owe it to my great company for introducing me to the greatest two and a half days of training I have ever—or will ever—have. YOU GUYS ROCK!
—*Hector A. Dilan*
Manager of Customer Logistics
Kraft/Nabisco, Inc. – Biscuit & Snack Division

I am sending you this note to let you know how pleased we are with all that you have done for our company. The individuals who have attended your classes have been raving about the results, and the work you have done with our shareholders has produced some amazing outcomes. Should you ever need us as a reference, please put us at the top of the list.
—*Grant D. "Butch" Anderson III*
Managing Shareholder, Muckell Anderson CPA

Who would have thought an analytical, skeptical control nut like me could have embraced such an unusual process? I am so thankful I did. I recommend *Leadership Awakening* to anyone who wants to stretch themselves. You'll find the man or woman you are designed to be. Each of my staff members has been given the opportunity to enroll in a *Leadership Awakening* class. I want them to become the parents, siblings, children and leaders they can be. I look forward to re-meeting each one of them.   —*April B. Box*
Vice President, Baylor Health Care System Foundation